ULSTER FOLKLORE

ULSTER FOLKLORE

ELIZABETH ANDREWS,

F . R . A . I .

BROWNSTONE BOOKS

A BROWNSTONE BOOK

Published by Wildside Press, LLC
www.wildsidebooks.com

CONTENTS

INTRODUCTION

In 1894 I was at the meeting of the British Association at Oxford, and had the good fortune to hear Professor Julius Kollmann give his paper on "Pygmies in Europe," in which he described the skeletons which had then recently been discovered near Schaffhausen. As I listened to his account of these small people, whose average height was about four and a half feet, I recalled the description of Irish fairies given to me by an old woman from Galway, and it appeared to me that our traditional "wee-folk" were about the size of these Swiss dwarfs. I determined to collect what information I could, and the result is given in the following pages. I found that the fairies are, indeed, regarded as small; but their height may be that of a well-grown boy or girl, or they may not be larger than a child beginning to walk. I once asked a woman if they were as small as cocks and hens, but she laughed at the suggestion.

I had collected a number of stories, and had become convinced that in these tales we had a reminiscence of a dwarf race, when I read some of Mr. David MacRitchie's works, and was gratified to find that the traditions I had gathered were in accordance with the conclusions he had drawn from his investigations in Scotland. A little later I made his acquaintance, and owe him many thanks for his great kindness and the encouragement he has given me in my work.

As will be seen in the following pages, tradition records several small races in Ulster: the Grogachs, who are closely allied to the fairies, and also to the Scotch and English Brownies; the short Danes, whom I am inclined to identify with the Tuatha de Danann; the Pechts, or Picts; and also the small Finns. My belief is that all these, including the fairies, represent primitive races of mankind, and that in the stories of women, children, and men being carried off by the fairies, we have a record of warfare, when stealthy raids were made and captives brought to the dark souterrain. These souterrains, or, as the country people call them, "coves," are very numerous. They are underground structures, built of rough stones without mortar, and roofed with large flat slabs. There is a fine one at Ardtole, near Ardglass, Co. Down. The total length of this souterrain is about one hundred and eight feet, its width three feet, and its height five feet three inches.[1]

As a rule, although the fairies are regarded as "fallen angels," they are said to be kind to the poor, and to possess many good qualities. "It was better for the land before they went away" is an expression I have heard more than once. The belief in the fairy changeling has, however, led to many acts of cruelty. We know of the terrible cases which occurred in the South of Ireland some years ago, and I met with the same superstition in the North. I was told a man believed his sick wife was not herself, but a fairy who had been substituted for her. Fortunately the poor woman was in hospital, so no harm could come to her.

Much of primitive belief has gathered round the

---

1   See "Ardtole Souterrain, Co. Down," by F. J. Bigger and W. J. Fennell in *Ulster Journal of Archæology*, 1898-99, pp. 146, 147.

fairy—we have the fairy well and the fairy thorn. It is said that fairies can make themselves so small that they can creep through keyholes, and they are generally invisible to ordinary mortals. They can shoot their arrows at cattle and human beings, and by their magic powers bring disease on both. They seldom, however, partake of the nature of ghosts, and I do not think belief in fairies is connected with ancestral worship.

Sometimes I have been asked if the people did not invent these stories to please me. The best answer to this question is to be found in the diverse localities from which the same tale comes. I have heard of the making of heather ale by the Danes, and the tragic fate of the father and son, the last of this race, in Down, Antrim, Londonderry, and Kerry. The same story is told in many parts of Scotland, although there it is the Picts who make the heather ale. I have been told of the woman attending the fairy-man's wife, acquiring the power of seeing the fairies, and subsequently having her eye put out, in Donegal and Derry, and variants of the story come to us from Wales and the Holy Land.

I am aware that I labour under a disadvantage in not being an Irish scholar, but most of those in Down, Antrim, and Derry from whom I heard the tales spoke only English, and in Donegal the peasants who related the stories knew both languages well, and I believe gave me a faithful version of their Irish tales.

Some of these essays appeared in the *Antiquary*, others were read to the Archæological Section of the Belfast Naturalists' Field Club, but are now published for the first time *in extenso*. All have been revised, and additional notes introduced. To these chapters on folklore I have added an article on the Rev. William Hamilton, who, in his "Letters on the North-East Coast of Antrim," written towards the close of the eighteenth century, gives an account of the geology, antiquities, and customs of the country.

The plan of the souterrain at Ballymagreehan Fort, Co. Down, was kindly drawn for me by Mr. Arthur Birch. I am much indebted to the Council of the Royal Anthropological Institute for their kindness in allowing me to reproduce the plan of the souterrain at Knockdhu from Mrs. Hobson's paper, "Some Ulster Souterrains," published in the *Journal* of the Institute, vol. xxxix., January to June, 1909. My best thanks are also due to Mrs. Hobson for allowing me to make use of her photograph of the entrance to this souterrain. The other illustrations are from photographs by Mr. Robert Welch, M.R.I.A., who has done so much to make the scenery, geology, and antiquities of the North of Ireland better known to the English public.

Belfast,
August, 1913.

FAIRIES AND THEIR DWELLING-PLACES[2]

In the following notes I have recorded a few traditions gathered from the peasantry in Co. Down and other parts of Ireland regarding the fairies. The belief is general that these little people were at one time very numerous throughout the country, but have now disappeared from many of their former haunts. At Ballynahinch I was told they had been blown away fifty years ago by a great storm, and the caretaker of the old church and graveyard of Killevy said they had gone to Scotland. They are, however, supposed still to inhabit the more remote parts of the country, and the old people have many stories of fairy visitors, and of what happened in their own youth and in the time of their fathers and grandfathers.

We must not, however, think of Irish fairies as tiny creatures who could hide under a mushroom or dance on a blade of grass. I remember well how strongly an old woman from Galway repudiated such an idea. The fairies, according to her, were indeed small people, but no mushroom could give them shelter. She described them as about the size of children, and as far as I can ascertain from inquiries made in many parts of Ulster and Munster, this is the almost universal belief among the peasantry. Sometimes I was told the fairies were as

---

2 Communicated to Belfast Naturalists' Field Club, January 18, 1898.

large as a well-grown boy or girl, sometimes that they were as small as children beginning to walk; the height of a chair or a table was often used as a comparison, and on one occasion an old woman spoke of them as being about the size of monkeys.

The colour red appears to be closely associated with these little people. In Co. Waterford, if a child has a red handkerchief on its head, it is said to be wearing a fairy cap. I have frequently been told of the small men in red jackets running about the forts; the fairy women sometimes appear in red cloaks; and I have heard more than once that fairies have red hair.

A farmer living in one of the valleys of the Mourne Mountains said he had seen one stormy night little creatures with red hair, about the size of children. I asked him if they might not have been really children from some of the cottages, but his reply was that no child could have been out in such weather.

An old woman living near Tullamore Park, Co. Down, described vividly how, going out to look after her goat and its young kid, she had heard loud screams and seen wild-looking figures with scanty clothing whose hair stood up like the mane of a horse. She spoke with much respect of the fairies as the gentry, said they formerly inhabited hills in Tullamore Park, and that care was taken not to destroy their thorn-bushes. She related the following story: As a friend of hers was sitting alone one night, a small old woman, dressed in a white cap and apron, came in and borrowed a bowl of meal. The debt was repaid, and the meal brought by the fairy put in the barrel. The woman kept the matter secret, and was surprised to find her barrel did not need replenishing. At last her husband asked if her store of meal was not coming to an end; she replied that she would show him she had sufficient, and lifted the cover of the barrel. To her astonishment it was almost empty; no doubt, had she kept her secret, she would have had an unlimited supply of meal.

I have heard several similar stories, and have not found that any evil consequences were supposed to follow from partaking of food brought by the fairies. Men have been carried off by them, have heard their beautiful music, seen them dancing, or witnessed a fairy battle without bringing any misfortune on themselves. On the other hand, according to a story I heard at Buncrana, Co. Donegal, a little herd-boy paid dearly for having entered one of their dwellings. As he was climbing among the rocks, he saw a cleft, and creeping through it came to where a fairy woman was spinning with her "weans," or children, around her. His sister missed him, and after searching for a time, she too, came to the cleft, and looking down saw her brother, and called to him to come out. He came, but was never able to speak again.

In another case deafness followed intercourse with the fairies. An elderly man at Maghera, Co. Down, told me that his brother when four or five years old went out with his father. The child lay down on the grass. After a while the father heard a great noise, and looking up saw little men about two feet in height dancing round his son. He called to them to be gone, and they ran towards a fort and disappeared. The child became deaf, and did not recover his hearing for ten years. He died at the age of seventeen.

To cut down a fairy thorn or to injure the house of a fairy is regarded as certain to bring misfortune. An old woman also living at Maghera, related how her great-grandmother had received a visit from a small old woman, who forbade the building of a certain turf-stack, saying that evil would befall anyone who injured the chimneys of her house. The warning was disregarded, the turf-stack built, and before long four cows died.

I was told that when a certain fort in Co. Fermanagh was levelled to the ground misfortune overtook the men who did the work, although, apparently, they were only labourers, many of them dying suddenly. It was also said that where this fort had stood there were caves or hollows in the ground into which the oxen would fall when ploughing. An attempt to bring a fort near Newcastle under cultivation is believed to have caused the sudden death of the owner.

The fairies are celebrated as fine musicians; they ride on small horses; the women grind meal, and the sound of their spinning is often heard at night in the peasants' cottages. The following story is related as having occurred at Camlough, near Newry.

A woman was spinning one evening when three fairies came into the house, each bringing a spinning-wheel. They said they would help her with her work, and one of them asked for a drink of water. The woman went to the well to fetch it. When there she was warned, apparently by a friendly fairy, that the others had come only to mock and harm her. Acting on the advice of this friend, the woman, as soon as she had given water to the three, turned again to the open door, and stood looking intently towards a fort. They asked what she was gazing at, and the reply was: "At the blaze on the fort." No sooner had she uttered these words than the three fairies rushed out with such haste that one of them left her spinning-wheel behind, which, according to the story, is now to be seen in Dublin Castle. The woman then shut her door, and put a pin in the keyhole, thus effectually preventing the return of her visitors.

In this story we have probably an allusion to the signal fires which are believed by the peasantry to have been lit on the forts in time of danger, one fort being always within view of another. These forts, or raths, appear to have been the favourite abode of the fairies. To use the language of the peasantry, these little people live in the "coves of the forths," an expression which puzzled me until I found that coves, or caves, meant underground passages—in other words, souterrains.

Plan of Ballymagreehan Souterrain.

There are a number of these souterrains in the neighbourhood of Castlewellan, and with a young friend, who helped me to take a few rough measurements, I explored several.

Ballymagreehan Fort is a short distance from Castlewellan, near the Newry Road. It is a small fort, and on the top we saw the narrow entrance to the souterrain. Passing down through this, we found ourselves in a short passage, or chamber, which led us to another passage at right angles to the first. It is about forty feet in length and three feet in width; the height varies from four to five feet. The roof is formed of flat slabs, and the walls are carefully built of round stones, but without mortar. At one end this passage appeared to terminate in a wall, but at the other it was only choked with fallen stones and débris, and I should think had formerly extended farther.

Herman's Fort is another small fort on the opposite side of Castlewellan, in the townland of Clarkill. Climbing to the top of it, we came to an enclosure where several thorn-bushes were growing. The farmer who kindly acted as our guide showed us two openings. One of these led to a narrow chamber fully six feet high, the other to a passage more than thirty feet in length and about three feet wide, while the height varied from three and a half feet in one part to more than five feet in another. I was told that water is always to be found near these forts, and was shown a well which had existed from time immemorial; the sides were built of round stones without mortar, in the same way as the walls of the passage.

We heard here of another souterrain about a mile

distant, called Backaderry Cove. It is on the side of a hill close to the road leading from Castlewellan to Dromara. A number of thorn-bushes grow near the place, but there is no mound, either natural or artificial. Creeping through the opening, we found ourselves in a passage about forty feet in length; a chamber opens off it nine feet in length, and between five and six feet in height, while the height of the passage varies from four and a half to five and a half feet. There is a tradition that this passage formerly connected Backaderry with Herman's Fort.

Ballyginney Fort is near Maghera. I only saw the entrance to the souterrain, but from what I heard I believe that here also there is a chamber opening off the passage. The farmer on whose land the fort is situated told me that one dry summer he had planted flax in the field adjoining the fort. The small depth of soil above the flat slabs affected the crop, so that by the difference in the flax it was easy to trace where the passage ran below the field.

We have seen that the fairies are believed to inhabit the souterrains; they are also said to live inside certain hills, and in forts where, so far as is known, no underground structure exists. I may mention as an example the large fort on the Shimna River, near Newcastle, where I was told their music was often to be heard. There may be many souterrains whose entrance has been choked up, and of which no record has been preserved. Mr. Bigger gave last session an interesting account of one discovered at Stranocum; another was accidentally found last September in a field about three miles from Newry. Mr. Mann Harbison, who visited the souterrain, writes to me that the excavation has been made in a circular portion which is six feet wide and five feet high. A gallery opens out of this chamber, and is in some places not more than three feet six inches high.

The building of the forts and souterrains is ascribed by the country people to the Danes, a race of whom various traditions exist. They are said to have had red hair; sometimes they are spoken of as large men, sometimes as short men. One old woman, who had little belief in fairies, told me that in the old troubled times in Ireland people lived inside the forts; these people were the Danes, and they used to light fires on the top as a signal from one fort to another. I heard from an elderly man of Danes having encamped on his grandmother's farm. Smoke was seen rising from an unfrequented spot, and when an uncle went to investigate the matter he found small huts with no doors, only a bundle of sticks laid across the entrance. In one of the huts he saw a pot boiling on the fire, and going forward he began to stir the contents. Immediately a red-haired man and woman rushed in; they appeared angry at the intrusion, and when he went out threw a plate after him.

The traditions in regard both to Danes and fairies are very similar in different parts of Ireland. In Co. Cavan the country people spoke of the beautiful music of the fairies, and told me of their living in a fort near

Lough Oughter. One woman said they were sometimes called Ganelochs, and were about the size of children, and an old man described them as little people about one or two feet high, riding on small horses.

In Co. Waterford I was told that the fairies were not ghosts: they lived in the air. One man might see them while they would be invisible to others.

In an interesting lecture on the "Customs and Superstitions of the Southern Irish," the Rev. J. B. Leslie, who has kindly allowed me to quote from his manuscript, describes the fairies as "a species of beings neither men nor angels nor ghosts.... They are connected in the popular imagination with the Danish forts which are common in the country. In these they seem to have their abode underground. At night they hold here high revels—in grand banqueting-halls— and in these revels there must always, I believe, be a living human being. The fairies are often called the 'good people'; some think they are 'fallen angels.' They are usually thought of as harmless creatures, unless, of course, they are interfered with, when the power they wield is very great. They are very fond of games; some testify that they have seen them play football, others hurley, while playing at marbles is a special pastime, and I have even heard of persons who have discovered 'fairy marbles' near or in these forts. No one will inter-fere with the forts; they fear the power and anger of the fairies."

While the fairies are generally associated with the forts, I heard both in Co. Down and Co. Kerry of their living in caves in the mountains, and a lad whom I met near the Gap of Dunloe described them as having cloven feet and black hair.

A boatman at Killarney spoke of the Leprechauns as little men about three feet in height, wearing red caps. He thought the fairies might be taller, and spoke of their living in the forts. He said these forts had been built by the Danes, who must have been small men, when they made the passages so low. We thus see that fairies and Danes are both associated with these ancient structures. Although the Irish peasant speaks of these Danes having been conquered by Brian Boru, the structure and position of the raths and souterrains point to their having been the work of one of the earlier Irish races rather than of the medieval Norsemen. Their name appears to identify them with the Tuatha de Danann whose necromantic power is celebrated in Irish tales, and of whom, according to O'Curry, one class of fairies are the representatives. I know that some high authorities regard the Tuatha de Danann and the fairies as alike mythological beings. The latter are certainly in popular legend endowed with superhuman attributes; they can transport people long distances, creep through keyholes, and the fairy changeling, when placed on the fire, can escape up the chimney and grin at his tormentors. If we ask the country people who are the fairies, the reply is frequently, "Fallen angels." According to an old woman in Donegal, these angels fell, some on the sea, some on the earth, while some remained in the air; the fairies were those who fell on the earth.

These "fallen angels" may be the representatives of the spirits whom the pagan Irish worshipped and strove to propitiate, and some of the tales relating to the fairies may have their origin in the mythology of a primitive people. But the raths and souterrains are certainly the work of human hands, and I would suggest that in the legends connected with them we have a reminiscence of a dwarf race who rode on ponies, were good musicians, could spin and weave, and grind corn. The traditions would point to their being red-haired.

Mr. Mann Harbison has kindly written to me on this subject, and expresses his belief that the souterrains "were constructed by a diminutive race, probably allied to the modern Lapps, who seem to be the survivors of a widely distributed race." In another letter he says: "The universal idea of fairies is very suggestive. The tall Celts, when they arrived, saw the small people disappear in a mysterious way, and, without stopping to investigate, imagined they had become invisible. If they had had the courage or the patience to investigate, they would have found that they had passed into their souterrain."

In his work "Fians, Fairies, and Picts," Mr. David MacRitchie argues that these three names belong to similar if not identical dwarf races in Scotland. The Tuatha de Danann he also regards as of the same race as the fairies, or, to give them their Irish name, the Fir Sidhe, the men of the green mounds.

The remains of the ancient cave-dwellers point to

a primitive race of small size inhabiting Europe. Dr. Munro, in his work "Prehistoric Problems," refers to the skeletons discovered at Spy in Belgium by MM. Lohest and De Pudzt. He describes them as examples of a very early and low type of the human race, and states that Professor Fraipont, who examined them anatomically, "came to the conclusion that the Spy men belonged to a race relatively of small stature, analogous to the modern Laplanders, having voluminous heads, massive bodies, short arms, and bent legs. They led a sedentary life, frequented caves, manufactured flint implements after the type known as Moustérien, and were contemporary with the Mammoth."[3]

Let us compare this description with that in the ballad of "The Wee, Wee Man":[4]

> *"His legs were scarce a shathmont's[5] length,*
> *And thick and thimber was his thigh;*
> *Between his brows there was a span,*
> *And between his shoulders there was three."*

I do not, however, mean to suggest that the builders of the raths and souterrains were contemporary with the men of Spy, but rather that a small race of primitive men may have existed until a comparatively late period in this country. Leading a desultory warfare with their

---

3   P. 141.

4   "Ancient and Modern Scottish Songs," published anonymously, but known to have been collected by David Herd (vol. i., p. 95, ed. 1776).

5   The fist closed with thumb extended, and may be considered a measure of about six inches.

neighbours, they would carry off women and children, and injure the cattle with their stone weapons. We should note that in the traditions of the peasantry, and also in the old ballads, those who have been carried off by the fairies can frequently be released from captivity, and they return, not as ghosts, but as living men or women. May we not see in these legends traces of a struggle between a primitive race, whose gods may have been, like themselves, of diminutive stature, and their more civilized neighbours, who accepted the teaching of the early Christian missionaries?

A DAY AT MAGHERA, CO. LONDONDERRY[6]

One fine morning last August I found myself in the quaint old town of Maghera. My first visit was to the post-office, where I bought some picture-cards, and inquired my way to Killelagh Church, the Cromlech, and the Sweat-house, as it is called, where formerly people indulged in a vapour-bath to cure rheumatism and other complaints. I was told to follow the main street. This I did, and when I came to the outskirts of the town I tried to get a guide, and spoke to a boy at one of the cottages. He, however, knew very little, but fortunately saw an elderly man coming down the road, who consented to show me the way, and proved an excellent guide. His name is Daniel McKenna, a coach-builder by trade. His father, who was teacher in Maghera National School for thirty-five years, knew Irish well, and I understand gave Dr. Joyce information in regard to some of the place-names in Co. Derry. Taking a road which led in a north-westerly direction, we came to the Cromlech, and a few yards farther on saw the old Church of Killelagh.

---

6   Read before the Archæological Section of the Belfast Naturalists' Field Club, January 15, 1913.

ENTRANCE TO SWEATHOUSE, MAGHERA.

My guide pointed out that the doorstep was much worn, doubtless by the feet of those who during many centuries had passed over it; he showed me, too, the strong walls, and said the mortar had been cemented with the blood of bullocks. This probably recalls an ancient custom, when an animal—in still earlier times it might be a human being[7]—was slain to propitiate or drive away the evil spirits and secure the stability of the building. A similar tradition exists in regard to Roughan Castle, the stronghold of Phelim O'Neill, in Co. Tyrone.

Leaving Killelagh Church, we continued our walk, and I asked my guide about the customs and tradi-

---

7 In "My Schools and Schoolmasters" (chap. x., pp. 222-223, ed. 1854), Hugh Miller describes the goblin who haunted Craig House, near Cromarty Firth, as a "grey-headed, grey-bearded, little old man," and the apparition was thus explained by a herdboy: "*Oh! they're saying* it's the spirit of the man that was killed on the foundation-stone just after it was laid, and then built intil the wa' by the masons, that he might keep the castle by coming back again; and *they're saying* that a' the verra auld houses in the kintra had murderit men builded intil them in that way, and that they have a' o' them this bogle."

tions of the country. He told me that on Hallow Eve Night salt is put on the heads of children to protect them from the fairies. These fairies, or wee folk, are about three feet in height, some not so tall; they are of different races or tribes, and have pitched battles at the Pecht's graveyard. This is a place covered with rough mounds and very rough stones, and is looked on as a great playground of the fairies; people passing through it are often led astray by them. The Pechts, or Picts, were described to me as having long black hair, which grew in tufts; they were small people, about four feet six inches in height, thick set, nearly as broad as they were long, strong in arms and shoulders, and with very large feet. When a shower of rain came on, they would stand on their heads and shelter themselves under their feet. Some years ago I was told a similar story in Co. Antrim of the Pechts lying down and using their feet as umbrellas.[8]

I regretted we had not time to visit a large fort we passed on the way to Ballyknock Farmhouse. Here we left the road, and, passing through some fields, came to the old Sweat-house. As you will see from the photograph kindly given to me by Mr. Lytle of Maghera, the entrance is on the side of a bank. It is a much more primitive structure than those at the Struel Wells, near Downpatrick. No mortar has been used in its construction, and I should say it is an old souterrain, or part of a souterrain. The following are rough measurements:

---

8   See next chapter.

Height of entrance	2	feet.
Width of entrance	15	inches.
Height of interior	5	feet 5 inches.
Width of interior	3	feet.
Length of interior	9	feet.

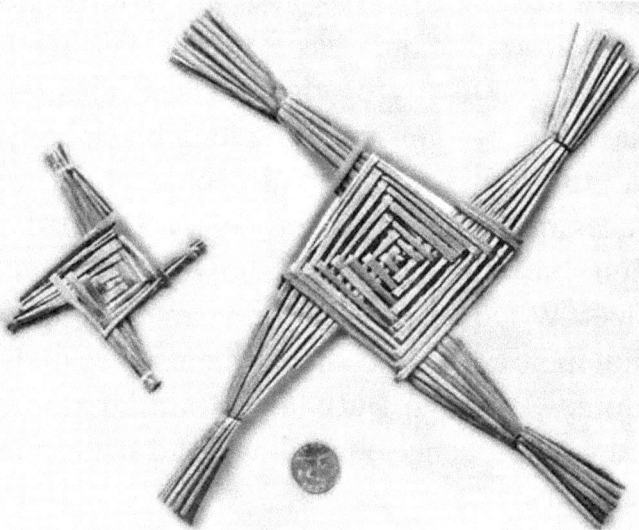

RUSH AND STRAW CROSSES.

This building, as already mentioned, was used by those suffering from rheumatism, and near the entrance is a well in which the patients bathed to complete the cure.

While we were resting I asked about rush crosses, which are put up in many cottages at Maghera, and, gathering some rushes, Daniel McKenna showed me how they were made. He told me that on St. Bridget's Eve, January 31, children are sent out to pull rushes, which must not be cut with a knife. When these rushes are brought in, the family gather round the fire and make the crosses, which are sprinkled with holy water. The wife or eldest daughter prepares tea and pancakes, and the plate of pancakes is laid on the top of the rush cross. Prayers are said, and the family partake of St. Bridget's supper. The crosses are hung up over doors and beds to bring good luck. In former times sowans or flummery was eaten instead of pancakes. I have heard of similar customs in other places. At Tobermore those who bring in the rushes ask at the door, "May St. Bridget come in?" "Yes, she may," is the answer. The rushes are put on a rail under the table while the family partake of tea. Afterwards the crosses are made, and, as at Maghera, hung up over doors and beds.[9]

This custom probably comes to us from pre-Christian times. The cross in its varied forms is a very ancient symbol, sometimes representing the sun, sometimes the four winds of heaven. Schlieman discovered it on the pottery of the Troad; it is found in Egypt, India, China, and Japan, and among the people of the Bronze Period it appears frequently on pottery, jewellery, and coins.

Now, St. Bridget had a pagan predecessor, Brigit, a poetess of the Tuatha de Danann, and whom we may perhaps regard as a female Apollo. Cormac, in his "Glossary," tells us she was a daughter of the Dagda and a goddess whom all poets adored, and whose two sisters were Brigit the physician and Brigit the smith. Probably the three sisters represent the same divine or semi-divine person whom we may identify with the

9   In the plate on the previous page, the larger cross is of rushes, the smaller one is made of straw.

British goddess Brigantia and the Gaulish Brigindo.

May we not see, then, in these rush crosses a very ancient symbol, used in pagan times, and which was probably consecrated by early Christian missionaries, and given a new significance?

HARVEST KNOTS.

The harvest knots or bows are connected with another old custom which was, until recently, observed at Maghera. When the harvest was gathered in, the last handful of oats, the corn of this country, was left standing. It was plaited in three parts and tied at the top, and was called by the Irish name "luchter." The reapers stood at some distance, and threw their sickles at the luchter, and the man who cut it was exempt from paying his share of the feast. Daniel McKenna told me he had seen some fine sickles broken in trying to hit the luchter. It was afterwards carried home; the young girls plaited harvest knots and put them in their hair, while the lads wore them in their caps and buttonholes. A dance followed the feast. The knots, with the ears of corn attached, are, I am told, the true old Irish type, while it is thought that the smaller ones were made after a pattern brought from England by the harvest reapers on their return home. I heard of the same custom at Portstewart and also in the Valley of the Roe, where the last sheaf of oats was called the "hare," and the throwing of the sickles was termed the "churn." In some places the last sheaf itself was called the "churn," but by whatever name it was known the man who hit it was regarded as the victor, and was given the best seat at the feast, or a reward of some kind. An old woman above ninety years of age repeated to me a song about the churn, or kirn, and she and many others remember well the custom and the feast which followed, when both whisky and tea were served.

In some districts the last sheaf is termed the "Cailleagh,"[10] or old wife.

A similar custom in Devonshire has been described by Mr. Pearse Chope in the *London Devonian Year Book* for 1910, p. 127. Here corn is wheat, and a sheaf of the finest ears, termed the "neck," is carried by one of the men to an elevated spot; the reapers form them-

---

10   Mr. McKean kindly informs me that he has found this name or its modification "Collya" in Counties Armagh, Monaghan, and Tyrone; also near Cushendall, Co. Antrim, where the ceremony is called "cutting the Cailleagh." He was told this Cailleagh was an old witch, and by "killing" her and taking her into the house you got good luck. At Ballyatoge, at the back of Cat Carn Hill, near Belfast, in the descent to Crumlin, the custom is called "cutting the Granny." At Ballycastle, Co. Antrim, the plait or braid is called the "car-line."

selves into a ring, and each man holding his hook above his head, they all join in "the weird cry, 'A neck! a neck! a neck! We ha' un! we ha' un! we ha' un!' This is repeated several times, with the occasional variation: 'A neck! a neck! a neck! God sa' un! God sa' un! God sa' un!' After this ceremony the man with the neck has to run to the kitchen, and get it there dry, while the maids wait with buckets and pitchers of water to 'souse' him and the neck." Mr. Chope adds that in most cases the neck is more or less in the form of a woman, and undoubtedly represented the spirit of the harvest, and that "the main idea of the ceremony seems to have been that in cutting the corn the spirit was gradually driven into the last handful.... As it was needful to cut the corn and bury the seed, so it was necessary to kill the corn spirit in order that it might rise again in fresh youth and vigour in the coming crop."[11]

I think we may safely assume that the Irish churn had a similar origin, and that in throwing the sickles the aim of the ancient reapers was to kill the spirit of the corn.

We have seen that in the North of Ireland the last sheaf is frequently termed the "hare," and in many other countries the corn spirit takes the form of an animal. In his recent volumes of the *Golden Bough*, entitled "Spirits of the Corn and the Wild," Dr. Frazer mentions many animals, such as the wolf, goat, fox, dog, bull, cow, horse, hare, which represent the corn

---

11   Dr. Frazer also describes this Devonshire custom (see *Golden Bough*, "Spirits of the Corn and the Wild," vol. i., pp. 264-267).

"CHURN"

spirit lurking in the last patch of standing corn. He tells us that "at harvest a number of wild animals, such as hares, rabbits, and partridges, are commonly driven by the progress of the reaping into the last patch of standing corn, and make their escape from it as it is being cut down.... Now, primitive man, to whom magical changes of shape seem perfectly credible, finds it most natural that the spirit of the corn, driven from his home in the ripe grain, should make his escape in the form of the animal, which is seen to rush out of the last patch of corn as it falls under the scythe of the reaper."[12]

To return to Maghera. The morning passed swiftly as I listened to my guide's description of these old customs, and it was after two o'clock when I said good-

12   "Spirits of the Corn and the Wild," vol. i., pp. 304, 305.

bye to him at his cottage, and found myself again in the main street of Maghera. I now wished to visit the Fort of Dunglady, and after a refreshing cup of tea, engaged a car. The driver knew the country well, and, going uphill and downhill, we passed through the village of Culnady, and were soon close to this fine fort. A few minutes' walk, and I stood on the outer ram part, and gazed across the inner circles at the cattle grazing on the central enclosure.

This fort was visited in 1902 by the Royal Society of Antiquaries of Ireland, when a very interesting paper, written by Miss Jane Clark of Kilrea, was read. She mentions that Dr. O'Donovan considered this fort one of the most interesting he had met with; not so magnificent as the Dun of Keltar at Downpatrick, but much better fortified, and states that a map of the time of Charles I. represents Dunglady Fort as a prominent object, and shows three houses built upon it, one of considerable size. Quoting from an unpublished letter of Mr. J. Stokes, she refers to the triple rampart, which makes the diameter of the whole to be three hundred and thirty feet. There was formerly a draw well in the middle of the fort, and at one time it was used as a burial-ground by members of the Society of Friends. Miss Clark also referred to a smaller fort at Culnady, which had been demolished. The two mounds in the centre of this rath had been formed of earth on a stone foundation.

A rapid drive brought me back to Maghera in time for a short visit to the ruins of the Church of St. Lurach, popularly known in the district as St. Lowry.

There is a curious sculpture of the Crucifixion over the west doorway, which is shown in the sketch of this doorway by Petrie in Lord Dunraven's "Notes on Irish Architecture."[13]

I must now conclude this account of my visit to Maghera, but may I mention that farther north there are other interesting antiquities? The large cromlech, called the Broadstone, is some miles from Kilrea. There are several forts in the neighbourhood of that town, which draws its supply of water from a fairy well.

---

13   Vol. i., p. 115.

ULSTER FAIRIES, DANES AND PECHTS[14]

The fairy lore of Ulster is doubtless dying out, but much may yet be learned about the "gentle" folk, and as we listen to the stories told by the peasantry, we may well ask ourselves what is the meaning of these old legends.

Fairies are regarded on the whole as a kindly race of beings, although if offended they will work dire vengeance. They have no connection with churchyards, and are quite distinct from ghosts. One old woman, who had much to say about fairies, when asked about ghosts, replied rather scornfully, that she did not believe in them. The fairies are supposed to be small—"wee folk"—but we must not think of them as tiny creatures who could hide in a foxglove. To use a North of Ireland phrase, they are the size of a "lump of a boy or girl!" and have been often mistaken for ordinary men or women, until their sudden disappearance marked them as unearthly.

A farmer in Co. Antrim told me that once when a man was taking stones from a cave in a fort, an old man came and asked him would it not be better to get his stones elsewhere than from those ancient buildings. The other, however, continued his work; but when the stranger suddenly disappeared, he became convinced that his questioner was no ordinary mortal.

---

14 Reprinted from the *Antiquary*, August, 1906.

In after-life he often said sadly: "He was a poor man, and would always remain a poor man, because he had taken stones from that cave." The cave was no doubt a souterrain.

An elderly woman in Co. Antrim told me that when a child she one evening saw "a little old woman with a green cloak coming over the burn." She helped her to cross, and afterwards took her to the cottage, where her mother received the stranger kindly, told her she was sorry she could not give her a bed in the house, but that she might sleep in one of the outhouses. The children made Grannie as comfortable as they could, and in the morning went out early to see how she was. They found her up and ready to leave. The child who had first met her said she would again help her across the burn—"But wait," she added, "until I get my bonnet." She ran into the house, but before she came out the old woman had disappeared.

When the mother heard of this she said: "God bless you, child! Don't mind Grannie; she is very well able to take care of herself." And so it was believed that Grannie was a fairy.

I have also heard of a little old man in a three-cornered hat, at first mistaken for a neighbour, but whose sudden disappearance proved him to be a fairy.

In the time of the press-gang a crowd was seen approaching some cottages. Great alarm ensued, and the young men fled; but it was soon discovered that these people did not come from a man-of-war—they were fairies.

A terrible story, showing how the fairies can punish their captives, was told me by an old woman at Armoy, in Co. Antrim, who vouched for it as being "candid truth." A man's wife was carried away by the fairies; he married again, but one night his first wife met him, told him where she was, and besought him to release her, saying that if he would do so she would leave that part of the country and not trouble him any more. She begged him, however, not to make the attempt unless he were confident he could carry it out, as if he failed she would die a terrible death. He promised to save her, and she told him to watch at midnight, when she would be riding past the house with the fairies; she would put her hand in at the window, and he must grasp it and hold tight. He did as she bade him, and although the fairies pulled hard, he had nearly saved her, when his second wife saw what was going on, and tore his hand away. The poor woman was dragged off, and across the fields he heard her piercing cries, and saw next morning the drops of blood where the fairies had murdered her.

Another woman was more fortunate; she was carried off by the fairies at Cushendall, but was able to inform her friends when she and the fairies would be going on a journey, and she told them that if they stroked her with the branch of a rowan-tree she would be free. They did as she desired. She returned to them, apparently having suffered no injury, and in the course of time she married.

This story was told me by a man ninety years of age,

living in Glenshesk, in the north of Co. Antrim. He spoke of the fairies as being about two feet in height, said they were dressed in green, and had been seen in daylight making hats of rushes. In Donegal I was also told that the fairies wore high peaked hats made of plaited rushes; but there, as in most parts of Ulster, and indeed of Ireland, the fairies are said to wear red, not green. In Antrim the fairies, like their Scotch kinsfolk, dress in green, but even there are often said to have red or sandy hair.

The Pechts are spoken of as low, stout people, who built some of the "coves" in the forts. An old man, living in the townland of Drumcrow, Co. Antrim, showed me the entrance to one of these artificial caves, and gave me a vivid description of its builders. "The Pechts," he said, "were low-set, heavy-made people, broad in the feet—so broad," he added, with an expressive gesture, "that in rain they could lie down and shelter themselves under their feet." He spoke of them as clad in skins, while an old woman at Armoy said they were dressed in grey. I have seldom heard of the Pechts beyond the confines of Antrim, although an old man in Donegal spoke of them as short people with large, unwieldy feet.

The traditions regarding the Danes vary; sometimes they are spoken of as a tall race, sometimes as a short race. There is little doubt that the tall race were the medieval Danes, while in the short men we have probably a reminiscence of an earlier race.

A widespread belief exists throughout Ireland that

the Danes made heather beer, and that the secret perished with them. According to an old woman at the foot of the Mourne Mountains, the Danes had the land in old times, but at last they were conquered, and there remained alive only a father and son. When pressed to disclose how the heather beer was made, the father said: "Kill my son, and I will tell you our secret"; but when the son was slain, he cried: "Kill me also, but our secret you shall never know!" I have the authority of Mr. MacRitchie for stating that a similar story is known in Scotland from the Shetlands to the Mull of Galloway, but there it is told of the Picts.

We all remember Louis Stevenson's ballad of heather ale—how the son was cast into the sea:

> "And there on the cliff stood the father,
> Last of the dwarfish men.
>
> "True was the word I told you:
> Only my son I feared;
> For I doubt the sapling courage
> That goes without the beard.
> But now in vain is the torture,
> Fire shall never avail;
> Here dies in my bosom
> The secret of heather ale."

The secret appears, however, to have been preserved for many centuries. After visiting Islay in 1772, the Welsh traveller and naturalist, Pennant, states that "Ale is frequently made in this island from the tops of heath, mixing two-thirds of that plant with one of malt."[15]

Probably these islanders were descendants of the Picts or Pechts.

I do not know if there is any record of the making of heather beer in Ireland in later times, but I heard the story of the lost secret in Down, in Kerry, in Donegal, in Antrim, and everywhere the father and the son were the last of the Danes. Does not this point to the Irish Danes being a kindred race to the Picts? If we may be allowed to hold that the Tuatha de Danann are not altogether mythical, I should be inclined to believe that they are the short Danes of the Irish peasantry, who built the forts and souterrains. I visited some Danes' graves near Ballygilbert, in Co. Antrim; it appeared to me that there were indications of a stone circle, the principal tomb was in the centre, the walls built without mortar, and I was told that formerly it had been roofed in with a flat stone. Various ridges were pointed out to me as marking the small fields of these early people. I was also shown their houses, built, like the graves, without mortar. Within living memory these old structures were much more perfect than at present, many of them having the characteristic flat slab as a roof; but fences were needed, and the Danes' houses offered a convenient and tempting supply of stones. In the same neighbourhood I was shown a building of uncemented stone with flat slabs

15 "Voyage to the Hebrides in 1772," p. 229. For a full discussion of the subject, see Mr. MacRitchie's "Memories of the Picts," in the *Scottish Antiquary* for 1900.

for the roof, and was told it had been built by the fairies.

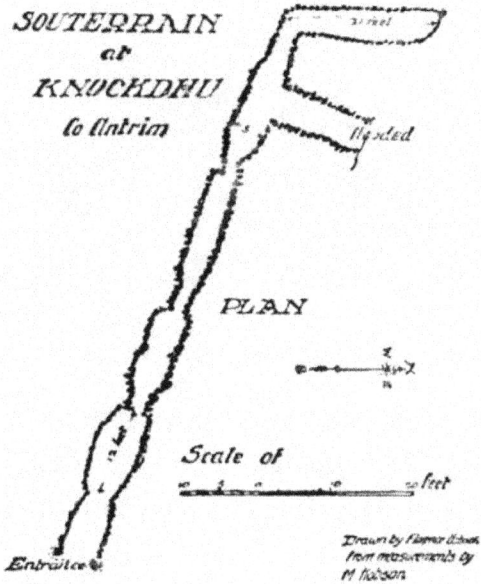

SOUTERRAIN at KNOCKDHU Co Antrim

PLAN

Scale of feet

Entrance

In the same district I visited a fine souterrain at the foot of Knockdhu, which was afterwards fully explored and measured by Mrs. Hobson. She describes it as "a souterrain containing six chambers, with a length of eighty-seven feet exclusive of a flooded chamber."[16] Mrs. Hobson photographed the entrance to this souterrain, which is reproduced on the next page.

16 See "Some Ulster Souterrains," *Journal of the Royal Anthropological Institute*, vol. xxxix., January-June, 1909. The plan was drawn by Miss Florence Hobson from the measurements made by Mrs. Hobson.

ENTRANCE TO SOUTERRAIN AT KNOCKDHU.

From the foregoing traditions it will be seen that Pechts, Danes, and fairies are all associated with the remains of primitive man. I may add that the small pipes sometimes turned up by the plough are called in different localities Danes', Pechts', or fairies' pipes.

The peasantry regard the Pechts and the Danes as thoroughly human; with the fairies it is otherwise. They are unearthly beings, fallen angels with supernatural powers; but, while quick to revenge an injury or a slight, on the whole friendly to mankind. "It was better for the country before they went away," was the remark made to me by an old woman from Garvagh, Co. Derry, and I have heard the same sentiment expressed by others. They are always spoken of with much respect, and are often called the "gentry" or the "gentle folk."

We hear of fairy men, fairy women, and fairy children. They may intermarry with mortals, and an old woman told me she had seen a fairy's funeral. Now, do these stories give us only a materialistic view of the spirit world held by early man, or can we also trace in them a reminiscence of a pre-Celtic race of small stature? The respect paid to the fairy thorn is no doubt a survival of tree-worship, and in the banshee we have a weird being who has little in common with mortal woman. On the other hand, the fairies are more often connected with the artificial Forts and souterrains than with natural hills and caves. These forts and souterrains, as we have seen, are also the habitations of Danes and Pechts. They are sacred spots—to injure them is to court misfortune; but I have not heard them spoken of as sepulchres.

I have already mentioned that I have rarely, if ever, found among the peasantry any tradition of fairies a few inches in height. In one of the tales in "Silva Gadelica" (xiv.) we read, however, of the lupracan being so small that the close-cropped grass of the green reached to the thigh of their poet, and the prize feat of their great champion was the hewing down of a thistle at a single stroke. Such a race could not have built the souterrains, and probably owe their origin to the imagination of the medieval story-teller. The lupracan were not, however, always of such diminutive size. In a note to this story Mr. Standish H. O'Grady quotes an old Irish manuscript[17] in which a distinctly human origin is ascribed to these luchorpan or wee-bodies. "Ham, therefore, was the first that was cursed after the Deluge, and from

---

17   Rawl., 486, f.49, 2.

him sprang the wee-bodies (pygmies), fomores, 'goat-heads' (satyrs), and every other deformed shape that human beings wear." The old writer goes on to tell us that this was the origin of these monstrosities, "which are not, as the Gael relate, of Cain's seed, for of his seed nothing survived the Flood."[18]

It is true that in this passage the lupracan or wee-bodies are associated with goatheads; but whether these are purely fabulous beings, or point to an early race whose features were supposed to resemble those of goats, or who perhaps stood in totem relationship to goats, it would be difficult to say. What we have here are two medieval traditions, the one stating that the pygmies are descendants of Cain, the other classing them among the descendants of Ham. Does the latter contain a germ of truth, and is it possible that at one time a people resembling the pygmies of Central Africa inhabited these islands?

Those who have visited the African dwarfs in their own haunts have been struck by the resemblance between their habits and those ascribed to the northern fairies, elves, and trolls.

Sir Harry Johnston states that anyone who has seen much of the merry, impish ways of the Central African pygmies "cannot but be struck by their singular resemblance in character to the elves and gnomes and sprites of our nursery stories." He warns us, however, against reckless theorizing, and says: "It may be too much to assume that the negro species ever inhabited Europe,"

---

18   "Silva Gadelica" (translation and notes), pp. 563, 564.

but adds that undoubtedly to his thinking "most fairy myths arose from the contemplation of the mysterious habits of dwarf troglodyte races lingering on still in the crannies, caverns, forests, and mountains of Europe after the invasion of neolithic man."[19] Captain Burroughs refers to the stories of these mannikins to be found in all countries, and adds that "it was of the highest interest to find some of them in their primitive and aboriginal state."[20] He speaks of the red and black Akka, and Sir Harry Johnston also describes the two types of pygmy, one being of a reddish-yellow colour, the other as black as the ordinary negro. In the yellow-skinned type there is a tendency on the part of the head hair to be reddish, more especially over the frontal part of the head. The hair is never absolutely black—it varies in colour between greyish-greenish-brown, and reddish.[21] We have seen how Irish fairies and Danes have red hair, but I should infer of a brighter hue than these African dwarfs. The average height of the pygmy man is four feet nine inches, of the pygmy woman four feet six inches,[22] and although we cannot measure fairies, I think the Ulster expression, "a lump of a boy or girl," would correspond with this height. I do not know the size of the fairy's foot, but, as we have seen, both Danes and Pechts have large feet, and so has the

---

19 "Uganda Protectorate," vol. ii., pp. 516, 517.

20 "Land of the Pygmies," pp. 173, 174.

21 "Uganda Protectorate," vol. ii. See pp. 527, 530; also coloured frontispiece.

22 "Uganda Protectorate," vol. ii., p. 532.

African pygmy[23] One of the great marks of the fairies is their vanishing and leaving no trace behind, and Sir Harry Johnston speaks of the baboon-like adroitness of the African dwarfs in making themselves invisible in squatting immobility.[24]

Dr. Robertson Smith has shown that "primitive man has to contend not only with material difficulties, but with the superstitious terror of the unknown, paralyzing his energies and forbidding him freely to put forth his strength to subdue nature to his use."[25] In speaking of the Arabian "jinn," he states "that even in modern accounts *jinn* and various kinds of animals are closely associated, while in the older legends they are practically identified,"[26] and he adds that the stories point distinctly "to haunted spots being the places where evil beasts walk by night."[27] He also shows that totems or friendly demoniac beings rapidly develop into gods when men rise above pure savagery,[28] and he cites the ancestral god of Baalbek, who was worshipped under the form of a lion.[29]

If we see, then, that early man, terrified by the wild beasts, whether lions or reptiles, ascribed to them superhuman powers, may not a similar mode of thought have caused one race to invest with supernatural attri-

23 *Ibid.*, p. 532.

24 *Ibid.*, p. 513.

25 "The Religion of the Semites," p. 115.

26 *Ibid.*, pp. 122, 123.

27 *Ibid.*, p. 123.

28 *Ibid.*, note *b*, p. 424.

29 *Ibid.*, p. 425.

butes another race, strangers to them, and possibly of inferior mental development? The big negro is often afraid to withhold his banana from the pygmy, and the dwarfish Lapps and Finns have long been regarded as powerful sorcerers by their more civilized neighbours. In like manner the little woman, inhabiting her underground dwelling at the foot of the sacred thorn-bush, might well be looked upon as an uncanny being, and in after-ages popular imagination might transform her into the weird banshee, the woman of the fairy mound, whose wailing cry betokens death and disaster.

FOLKLORE CONNECTED WITH ULSTER RATHS AND SOUTERRAINS[30]

As the title of this paper I have given "Folklore connected with Ulster Raths and Souterrains," but if I used the language of the country-people I should speak, not of raths and souterrains, but of forths and coves. In these coves it is believed the fairies dwell, and here they keep as prisoners women, children, even men. These subterranean dwellings may not be known to mortals. I heard of a lad being kept for several days in the fort of the Shimna, near Newcastle, Co. Down, and I was told that the great rath at Downpatrick had been a very gentle place, meaning one inhabited by fairies. In neither of these forts is there, as far as is known, a souterrain, nor is there one in the old fort at Antrim, a typical rath. In many cases we do find the entrance to a souterrain is in a fort. I may mention Ballymagreehan Fort, the stone fort near Altnadua Lough in Co. Down, and Crocknabroom, near Ballycastle. Although not in Ulster, I may also refer to a fine example of a rath with a souterrain in it, the Mote of Greenmount, described by the Rev. J. B. Leslie in his "History of Kilsaran, Co. Louth."[31]

---

30   Read before the Archæological Section of the Belfast Naturalists' Field Club, February 12, 1908.

31   Pp. 12-20. Several sections of this rath are given; also a view

THE OLD FORT, ANTRIM.

Many souterrains have no fort above them. Take, for example, the one near Scollogstown, Co. Down, with its numerous bridges, which it would be decidedly unpleasant to face if little men were behind them shooting arrows. Also Cloughnabrick Cave, near Ballycastle, which is not built with stones, but hollowed out of the basaltic rock.

Fairies are not the only race connected with raths and souterrains. We have two others, Danes and Pechts. It is generally believed that the Danes built the forts; hence we find many of them called "Danes' forts." I will describe one named from the townland in which it is situated, Ballycairn Fort. It stands on a high bank overlooking the Bann, about a mile north of Coleraine. The entire height is about twenty-six feet; at perhaps

showing Greenmount in 1748, and a plan of the same date—both from Wright's "Louthiana," published in that year.

twelve feet from the ground a flat platform is reached, and at one end of this the upper part of the fort rises in a circular form for about fourteen or fifteen feet. I was told the Danes who built it were short, stout people, and as they had no wheelbarrows they carried the earth in their leathern aprons. Here we seem to come in contact with a very primitive people, probably wearing the skins of wild animals, and who are said, like the fairies, to have sandy or red hair.

As far as is known no souterrain exists in Ballycairn Fort, although I was shown a stone at the side which my guide said might be the entrance to a "cove"; it appeared to me to be simply a piece of rock appearing above the sod, or possibly a boulder. There is a tradition of fairies living in this fort, as it is said that in "long ago" times the farmers used to threaten their boys if they were not doing right, that the fairies would come out of the fort and carry them away.

Many of the souterrains in this part of the world are now blocked up, and of some the entrance is no longer known, although they have been explored within living memory; others have been destroyed. There was a souterrain a short distance from Ballycairn fort in a field opposite to Cranogh National School. The master of this school told me that fifteen or sixteen years ago these underground buildings existed, but now they have been all quarried away. He also mentioned a tradition that there was a subterranean passage under the Bann.

On the opposite bank of the river, near Portstewart, I heard of several of these underground dwellings.

One was on the land of an old farmer eighty-four years of age. He told me he had been in this cave, but no one could get in now. It had been hollowed out by man, but the walls were not built of stones. There were several rooms; you dropped from one to another through a narrow hole. The rooms were large, but low in the roof; in one of them a quantity of limpet-shells were found. He added that some said that the Danes had built these caves, others that the clans made them as places of refuge. He added that the Danes of those days had sandy hair and were short people; not like the sturdy Danes of the present day. These are well known to the seafaring population of Ulster, and we sometimes find the old Danes spoken of as a tall, fair race; probably this is a true description of the medieval sea-rovers. The short Danes I should be inclined to identify with the Tuatha de Danann, and I believe that, notwithstanding the magical portents which abound in the tales that have come down to us, we have here a very early people who had made some progress in the arts.

This double use of the name Dane seems at times to have perplexed the older writers. The Rev. William Hamilton, in his "Letters on the North-East Coast of Antrim," published towards the end of the eighteenth century, gives a description of the coal-mines of Ballycastle[32] and of the very ancient galleries, with the pillars, left by the prehistoric miners, supporting the roof, which had been discovered some twelve years

---

32   Read before the Archæological Section of the Belfast Naturalists' Field Club, February 12, 1908.

before he wrote. He tells us that the people of the place ascribed them to the Danes, but argues that these were never peaceable possessors of Ireland, and that it is not "to the tumultuary and barbarous armies of the ninth and tenth centuries ... we are to attribute the slow and toilsome operations of peace." He mentions how the stalactite pillars found in these galleries marked their antiquity, and ascribes them to some period prior to the eighth century, "when Ireland enjoyed a considerable share of civilization."

In the same way John Windele, writing in the *Ulster Journal of Archæology* for 1862, speaks of the mines in Waterford having been worked by the ancient inhabitants, and adds: "One almost insulated promontory is perforated like a rabbit-burrow, and is known as the 'Danes' Island,' the peasantry attributing these ancient mines, like all other relics of remote civilisation, to the Danes."[33]

From my own experience I can corroborate this statement. An artificial island in Lough Sessiagh, in Co. Donegal, was shown to me as the work of the Danes. The forts on Horn Head and at Glenties are also ascribed to them.

The use of the souterrains was not confined to prehistoric times. The one at Greenmount appears to have been inhabited by the medieval Danes, as a Runic inscription, engraved on a plate of bronze, has been discovered in it, the only one as yet found

33   Pp. 12-20. Several sections of this rath are given; also a view showing Greenmount in 1748, and a plan of the same date—both from Wright's "Louthiana," published in that year.

in Ireland. In 1317 every man dwelling in an ooan, or caher's souterrain, was summoned to join the army of Domched O'Brian.[34] The French traveller, Jorevin de Rocheford, speaks of subterranean vaults where the peasants assembled to hear Mass,[35] and in still more recent times the smuggler and the distiller of illicit whisky found them convenient places of concealment.

In a former paper I referred to the lost secret of the heather beer, and the tragic ending of the last of the Danes.[36] As the story was told me near Ballycairn Fort, the father said: "Give my son the first lilt of the rope, and I will reveal our secret"; but when the son was dead the father cried: "Slay me also, for none shall ever know how the heather beer was brewed!"

In a paper read to this club Mr. McKean[37] mentioned that this story had been told to him in Kerry, where I, too, heard it. It appears to be almost universal in Ulster. When visiting Navan Fort, the ancient Emania, near Armagh, I was told that on this fort the Danes made heather beer. I asked if any heather grew in the neighbourhood, but the answer was, not now. There are variants of the tale. In some parts of Donegal it is wine, not beer, that the Danes are said to have made. As a rule the slaughter is taken for granted, and very little said

---

34 Part I., Letter IV., Edition 1822.

35 See "Illustrations of Irish History," by C. Litton Falkiner, p. 416. He considers it probable that Jorevin de Rochefort was Albert Jouvin de Rochefort, Trésorier de France.

36 *Ulster Journal of Archæology*, 1861-62, p. 212.

37 See Annual Report of Belfast Naturalists' Field Club, 1907-08, "A Holiday Trip to West Kerry," p. 73.

about it; but a farmer in Co. Antrim gave me a full account of the massacre, how at a great feast a Roman Catholic sat beside each Dane, and at a given signal plunged his dirk into his neighbour's side, until only one man and his son remained alive; then followed the usual sequel.

These short Danes are said to have had large feet, and one man described their arms as so long that they could pick anything off the ground without stooping. Long arms are also a characteristic of the traditional dwarf of Japan, probably an ancestor of the Aino.[38] As I mentioned in a previous paper,[39] large feet are also a traditional characteristic of the Pechts, who are generally said to have been clad in skins or in grey clothes. They have occasionally superhuman attributes ascribed to them. The same man who spoke of the long arms of the Danes said the Pechts could creep through keyholes—they were like "speerits"—and he evidently regarded both them and the fairies as evil spirits. At the same time he said they would thresh corn or work for a man, but if they were given food, they would be offended, and go away.

I think the close connection between Danes, Pechts, and fairies will be apparent to all, although the fairy has more supernatural characteristics, and in the banshee assumes a very weird form. Lady Fanshawe has described the apparition she saw when staying,

38   See Mr. David MacRitchie's "Northern Trolls," read at the Folklore Congress, Chicago, 1893, p. 12.

39   See "Memoirs of Anne, Lady Fanshawe," edited by Herbert C. Fanshawe, pp. 57-59.

in 1649, with the Lady Honora O'Brien, as a woman in white, with red hair and ghastly complexion, who thrice cried "Ahone!" and vanished with a sigh more like wind than breath. This was apparently the ghost of a murdered woman, who was said to appear when any of the family died, and that night a cousin of their hostess had passed away.[40] Similar stories, as we all know, exist at the present day.

Except in the case of the banshee, fairies rarely partake of the nature of ghosts, and I should note that in her description of the apparition Lady Fanshawe does not use the word "banshee." In many respects the fairies are akin to mortals—there are fairy men, fairy women, and fairy children. Fairies often live under bushes, and I was told in Co. Armagh that it would be a very serious matter to cut down a "lone" thorn-bush; those growing in rows were evidently less sacred. Did the thorn-bush hide the entrance to the subterranean dwelling?

The fairies are quick to revenge an injury or an encroachment on their territory. A fire which occurred at Dunree on Lough Swilly was attributed to the fairies, who were supposed to be angry because the military had carried the works of their modern fort too near the fairy rock. In some places the raths have been cultivated, but, as a rule, this is looked upon as very unlucky, and sure to bring dire misfortune on the man who attempts it. On the other hand, there appears to be no objection to growing crops on the top of a

---

40   See "Memoirs of Anne, Lady Fanshawe," edited by Herbert C. Fanshawe, pp. 57-59.

souter rain. Many are, it is true, afraid to enter these dark abodes, and others consider it unwise to carry anything out of them. I have never heard them spoken of as tombs, and the fairies are regarded, not as ghosts, but as fallen angels, to whom no Church holds out a hope of salvation. Only in one instance did a woman tell me that as fairies were good to the poor, she thought there would be hope for them hereafter. The Irish fairy remains a pagan; the ancient well of pre-Christian days may be consecrated to the Christian saint, and patterns held beside it, but no pious pilgrim prays on the rath or below the fairy rock.

We may now ask ourselves the meaning of these legends. The rath and souterrain are undoubtedly the work of primitive man, yet here we have the Sidh, inhabited by the fairy and the Tuatha de Danann. In the "Colloquy of the Ancients"[41] we are told it was out of a Sidh, Finn's chief musician, the dwarf Cnu deiriol came, and from another Sidh came Blathnait, whom the small man espoused. It was fairy music which Cnu taught to the musicians of the Fianna. It was out of a Sidh in the south that Cas corach, son of the Olave of the Tuatha de Danann, came to the King of Ulidia.[42]

In Derrick's "Image of Ireland," written in 1578, and published in 1581, the Olympian gods call upon certain little mountain gods, whom I should be inclined to

---

41   See "Memoirs of Anne, Lady Fanshawe," edited by Herbert C. Fanshawe, pp. 57-59.

42   Translated by Mr. S. H. O'Grady in "Silva Gadelica," volume with translation and notes. (For Cnu and Blathnait, see pp. 115-117.)

identify with the fairies, to come to their aid:

> *"Let therefore little Mountain Gods*
> *A troupe (as thei maie spare)*
> *Of breechlesse men at all assaies,*
> *Both leauvie and prepare*
> *With mantelles down unto the shoe*
> *To lappe them in by night;*
> *With speares and swordes and little dartes*
> *To shield them from despight.'*[43]

May I, in conclusion, express my belief that in the traditions of fairies, Danes, and Pechts the memory is preserved of an early race or races of short stature, but of considerable strength, who built underground dwellings, and had some skill in music and in other arts? They appear to have been spread over a great part of Europe. It is possible that, as larger races advanced, these small people were driven southwards to the mountains of Switzerland, westward towards the Atlantic, and northward to Lapland, where their descendants may still be found. No doubt there is a large supernatural element, especially in the stories of the fairies; but the same may be said of the tales of witches in the seventeenth century. The witch was undoubtedly human, yet she was believed, and sometimes believed herself, to possess superhuman powers, and to be in communication with un earthly beings. We must also remember the widespread belief in local spirits or gods, and a taller race of invaders might well

---

43   P. 38, Edinburgh, 1883; edited by John Small, M.A., F.S.A.Scot.

fear the magic of an earlier people long settled in the country, even if the latter were inferior in bodily and mental characteristics.

TRADITIONS OF DWARF RACES IN IRELAND AND IN SWITZERLAND[44]

In the traditions alike of Switzerland and of Ireland we hear of a dwarfish people, dwellers in mountain caves or in artificial souterrains, who are gifted with magical powers. The quaint figure of the Swiss dwarf with his peaked cap has been made familiar to us by the carvings of the peasantry, and in Antrim and Donegal the Irish fairy is said to wear a peaked cap of plaited rushes. With rushes he also makes a covering for his feet.[45]

Closely allied to the fairy is the Grogach, with his large head and soft body, who appears to have no bones as he comes tumbling down the hills. These Grogachs I heard of in North-East Antrim, and in them, as in the fairies, the supernatural characteristics preponderate. I was told that both were full of magic, and had come from Egypt.

---

44   Reprinted from the *Antiquary*, October, 1909.

45   May it not be that Cinderella's glass shoe was really green and derived its name from the Irish word *glas*, denoting that colour, which is familiar to us in place-names? I make this conjecture with diffidence. I know the usual explanation is that the shoe was made of a kind of fur called in Old French *vair*, and that a transcriber changed this word into *verre*. Miss Cox, in her "Cinderella," mentions that she had only found six instances of a glass shoe. As Littré says in the article on *vair* in his Dictionary, a *soulier de verre* is absurd. A fur slipper, however, does not appear very suitable for a ball.

We have, however, two other small races who are usually regarded by the peasantry as strictly human, the Pechts and the Danes.[46] Two traditions regarding Danes exist: sometimes we hear of tall Danes, doubtless the medieval sea-rovers; sometimes of small Danes, the builders of many of the raths and souterrains.

While the Danes are the great builders throughout Ireland, some of the raths and souterrains, especially those in North-East Antrim, are said to have been made by the Pechts. Last summer I visited one of these, the cave of Finn McCoul. It is a souterrain situated in Glenshesk, about three miles from Ballycastle. The ground above it is perfectly flat, no fort or any inequality to mark the spot; indeed, the farmer who kindly opened it for me had at first a difficulty in knowing in what part of the field to dig, as the entrance had been covered. On my second visit, however, I found he had discovered the spot. Entering a narrow passage, I crept through an opening from one and a half to two feet high, and found myself in a narrow chamber eight or nine feet long and little over four feet in height. The roof was formed of large flat slabs, which I was told were whinstone (basalt). At the opposite end of this chamber there was another narrow opening, leading, I presume, to a passage. I did not, however, venture farther; but I understand this artificial cave extends for about twenty perches underground, and has several chambers.

---

46   See Ulster Fairies, Danes and Pechts, p. 27 *et seq.*

GREY MAN'S PATH, FAIR HEAD.

I was told that this cave was the hiding-place of Finn McCoul. His garden was pointed out to me on rising ground at some little distance, and I was also informed that about fifty years ago his castle stood on the hill; but nothing now remains of it, the stones having been used when roads were made.

The following story was related to me on the spot: A Scotch giant came over to fight Finn McCoul, but was conquered and slain. To celebrate this victory Finn invited the Grey Man of the Path to a feast; but as hares and rabbits would have been too small to furnish a repast for this giant, Finn took his dog and went out to hunt red deer. They were unsuccessful, and in anger he slew his dog Brown,[47] which afterwards caused him much sorrow.

In the Grey Man of the Path we have, doubtless, a purely mythical character, an impersonation of the

47   This is, no doubt, a corruption of Bran.

mists which gather round Benmore,[48] while Finn McCoul, or MacCumaill, is one of Ireland's greatest traditional heroes. According to a well-known legend, he was a giant, and united Scotland and Ireland by a stupendous mole, of which the cave at Staffa and the Giant's Causeway are the two remaining fragments. In Glenshesk he is only a tall man, between seven and eight feet in height. Sometimes he is said to have been chief of the Pechts; sometimes he is spoken of as their master, and it is said they worked as slaves to him and the Fians.

According to tradition, the Pechts were very numerous, and must have carried the heavy slabs for the roof of Finn McCoul's cave a distance of several miles. Although usually looked on as strictly human, supernatural characteristics are sometimes attributed to them. Like the Swiss "Servan," both they and the Grogachs have been known to thresh corn or do other work for the farmers.

I was told at Ballycastle of one man who always laid out at night the bundles of corn he expected the Grogach to thresh, and each morning the appointed task was accomplished. One night he forgot to lay the corn on the floor of the barn, and threw his flail on the

---

48   The Grey Man's Path is a fissure on the face of Benmore or Fair Head, by which a good climber can ascend the cliff. It has been suggested that this Grey Man is one of the old gods, possibly Manannan, the Irish sea-god. In the *Ulster Journal of Archæology* for 1858, vol. vi., p. 358, there is an account given of the Grey Man appearing near the mouth of the Bush River to two youths, who believed they would have seen his cloven foot had he not been standing in the water. They had at first mistaken the apparition for an ordinary man.

top of the stack. The poor Grogach imagined that he was to thresh the whole, and set to work manfully; but the task was beyond his strength, and in the morning he was found dead. The farmer and his wife buried him, and mourned deeply the loss of their small friend.

Clough-na-murry Fort is said to be a "gentle"[49] place, yet an old man living near it told me he did not believe in the Grogachs; he thought it was the Danes who had worked for the farmers. He said these Danes were a persevering people, and that when they were in distress they would thresh corn for the farmers, if food were left out for them. Others say that the Danes were too proud to work.

One does not hear much of Brownies in Ulster; but I have been told they were hairy people who did not require clothes, but would thresh or cut down a field of corn for a farmer. On one occasion, out of gratitude for the work done, some porridge was left for them on plates round the fire. They ate it, but went away crying sadly:

> *"I got my mate an' my wages,*
> *An' they want nae mair o' me."*

Although, according to some, the Grogachs gladly accept food, others say that they and the Pechts are offended if it is offered to them, and leave to return no more.

I have not often heard of clothes being offered to the Pechts or Grogachs, but the Rev. John G. Campbell

---

49   A place inhabited by fairies, or "gentlefolk."

relates a story of a Brownie in Shetland who ground grain in a hand-quern at night. He was rewarded for his labours by a cloak and hood left for him at the mill. These disappeared in the morning, and with them the Brownie, who never came back.[50]

A similar tale is told of a Swiss dwarf. At Ems, in Canton Valais, a miller engaged the services of a "Gottwerg," and the little man worked early and late, sometimes rising in the night to see that all was in order. The mill produced twice as much as formerly, and at the end of the year the dwarf was rewarded by a garment made of the best wool. He put it on, jumped for joy, and crying out, "Now I am a handsome man, I have no more need to grind rye," he disappeared, and was not seen again.[51]

In these tales from Ireland, Scotland, and Switzerland, may there not be a reminiscence of a conquered race of small stature, but considerable strength, who worked either as slaves or for some small gift? No doubt they were badly fed, and their clothing would be of the scantiest.

Like the Danes and the Pechts, the fairies live underground. There is a widespread story of a fairy woman who begs a cottager not to throw water out at the doorstep, as it falls down her chimney. The request is invariably granted.

Some of these "wee folk" dwell in palaces under the

---

50   "Superstitions of the Highlands and Islands of Scotland," p. 188.

51   Dr. J. Jegerlehner, "Was die Sennen erzählen, Märchen und Sagen aus dem Wallis," pp. 102, 103.

sea. I heard a story at Ballyliffan, in Co. Donegal, of men being out in a boat which was nearly capsized by a heavy sea raised by a fairy. At last one sailor cried out to throw a nail against the advancing wave; this was done, and the nail hit the fairy. That night a woman, skilled in healing, received a message calling upon her to go to the courts below the sea. She consented, extracted the nail, and cured the fairy woman, but was careful not to eat any food offered to her. This fairy is said to have promised a man a pot of gold if he would marry her, but he refused.

An old man at Culdaff told me another tale of the sea. A fishing-boat was nearly overwhelmed, when a fairy-boat was seen riding on the top of a great wave, and a voice from it cried: "Do not harm that boat; an old friend of mine is in it." The voice belonged to a man who was supposed to be dead; but he had been carried off by the fairies, and would not allow them to injure his old friend.

If the Irish fairy has power over the waves, the Swiss dwarf can divert the course of the devastating landslip. I was told by an elderly man in the Bernese Oberland of the destruction of Burglauenen, a village near Grindelwald. All the cottages were overwhelmed by a landslip except one poor hut, which had given shelter to a dwarf, who was seen, seated on a stone, directing the moving mass away from the abode of his friends. A similar story is told of the destruction of Niederdorf, in the Simmenthal.[52] One Sunday evening

---

52   See "Der Untergang des Niederdorfs" in "Sagen und Sagengeschichten aus dem Simmenthal," vol. ii., pp. 29-44, by

a feeble little man clad in rags came to the village; he knocked at several houses, praying the inmates to give him, for the love of God, a night's shelter. Everywhere he was refused—one hard-hearted woman telling him to go and break stones—until he came to a poor basket-maker and his wife, who gave him the best they had, and when he left he promised that God would reward them. A week later the village was destroyed by a terrible landslip, but here also the dwarf saved the dwelling of those who had befriended him.

In this story and in many others the Swiss dwarf appears as a good Christian, but sometimes a rude and terrible form of paganism is attributed to him. In the tale of the "Gotwergini im Lötschental"[53] these dwarfs are accused of devouring children, and are said to have buried an old woman alive. She was apparently one of themselves. When they were laying her in the pit she wept bitterly, and begged that she might go free, saying she could still cook. But the dwarfs showed no pity: placing some bread and wine beside her, they covered in the grave. Is this an instance of the primitive barbarism of killing those no longer able to work, which is said still to exist among the Todas of India, and of which traces have been found in the customs of Scandinavia and other countries?[54]

D. Gempeler.

53   See "Am Herdfeuer der Sennen, Neue Märchen und Sagen aus dem Wallis," pp. 26-31, by Dr. J. Jegerlehner.

54   See "Folklore as an Historical Science," by Sir G. Laurence Gomme, pp. 67-78.

The Irish fairy never appears as a Christian.[55] He is regarded by the peasant as a fallen angel, and no Church holds out to him the hope of salvation. I was told in Inishowen that a priest walking between Clonmany and Ballyliffan was surrounded by the "wee folk," who asked anxiously if they could be saved. He threw his book towards them, bade them catch it, and he would give them an answer; but at the sight of the breviary they scattered and fled.[56]

The Protestant Bible and hymn-book are equally dreaded by them, and are used as a spell against their influence. I was told in the North of Antrim of a woman who was nearly carried off by the fairies because her friends had omitted to leave these books beside her. Luckily her husband, who was sleeping by the fire, awoke in time to save her. A pair of scissors, a darning-needle, or any piece of iron, would have been efficacious as a charm, so would the husband's trousers, if thrown across the bed.

While, as we have seen, the fairies are endowed with many supernatural qualities, they have much in

---

55   I have heard of only one exception.

56   Patrick Kennedy, in "A Belated Priest," tells how the "good people" surrounded a priest on a dark night, and asked him to declare that at the Last Day their lot would not be with Satan. He replied by the question, "Do you adore and love the Son of God?" There came no answer but weak and shrill cries, and with a rushing of wings the fairies disappeared (see "Fictions of the Irish Celts," p. 89). In "The Priest's Supper," the good people are anxious to know if their souls will be saved at the Last Day, but when an interview with a priest is suggested to them they fly away (see "Fairy Legends and Traditions of the South of Ireland," by T. Crofton Croker, pp. 36-42).

common with ordinary mortals; there are fairy men, fairy women, and fairy children. I have more than once heard of a fairy's funeral; they intermarry with mortals, and I have been told that those who bear the name of Ferris are descended from fairies. I presume Ferris is a corruption of Fir Sidhe. Fairies are never associated with churchyards, nor are they usually looked on as the spirits of the departed. The banshee may, indeed, partake to some extent of a ghostly character. Lady Wilde speaks of her as the "spirit of death— the most weird and awful of all the fairy powers," and adds, "but only certain families of historic lineage or persons gifted with music and song are attended by this spirit."[57]

It has often been stated that the banshee is an appanage of the great, but this is not the belief of the peasantry of Ulster: many families in humble life have a banshee attached to them. When in a curragh on Lough Sessiagh, in Co. Donegal, the neighbouring hill of Ben Olla was pointed out to me, and I was also shown a small cottage in which a girl named Olla had lived. She was carried off by the fairies, and her wailing was heard before the death of her mother, and again before the death of several members of her family. A farmer, or even a labourer, may have a banshee attached to his family—a little white creature was the description given to me by a woman who said she had seen one; others say that banshees are like birds.

To leave these weird apparitions, it will be seen that

---

57   "Ancient Legends, Mystic Charms, and Superstitions of Ireland," vol. i., p. 250.

the ordinary fairy, the Grogach, the Pecht, and the Dane, all inhabit underground dwellings, although the fairy and Grogach are regarded more in the light of supernatural beings. To cut down a fairy or a "Skiough" bush is to court misfortune, sometimes to attempt an impossible task. In Glenshesk some men tried to cut down a Skiough bush, but the hatchet broke; after several failures they gave up, and the bush still flourishes. Another bush was transplanted, but returned during the night.

To the Danes and Pechts the building of all the raths and souterrains is ascribed, and in North-East Antrim the Pechts are said to have been so numerous that, when making a fort, they could stand in a long line, and hand the earth from one to another, no one moving a step. A similar story is told of the Scotch Pechts by the Rev. Andrew Small in his "Antiquities of Fife" (1823).[58] Speaking of the Round Tower of Abernethy, "The story goes," he says, "that it was built by the Pechts ... and that while the work was going on they stood in a row all the way from the Lomond Hill to the building, handing the stones from one to another.... That it has been built of freestone from the Lomond Hill is clear to a demonstration, as the grist or nature of the stone points out the very spot where it has been taken from—namely, a little west, and up from the ancient wood of Drumdriell, about a mile straight south from Meralsford." According to popular tradition in Scotland, these Pechts or Picts were great builders,

---

58   It is quoted by Mr. David MacRitchie in "Testimony of Tradition," p. 67.

and many of the edifices ascribed to them belong to a comparatively late period. Mr. MacRitchie suggests that in the erection of some of these the Picts may have been employed as serfs or slaves.[59] He believes the Pechts to be the Picts of history. Mr. W. C. Mackenzie, on the other hand, has suggested that they are an earlier dwarf race, the Pets or Peti, who have been confused by the peasantry with the Picts.[60] This is a matter I must leave to others to decide; but I may remark in passing that in an ancient poem on the Cruithnians, preserved in the book of Lecan, we have a suggestion that these Cruithnians or Picts were a smaller race than their enemies, the Tuath Fidga. We are told how

"God vouchsafed unto them, in munificence,
For their faithfulness—for their reward—
To protect them from the poisoned arms
Of the repulsive horrid giants."[61]

Then follows an account of the cure discovered by the Cruithnian Druid—how he milked thrice fifty cows into one pit, and bathing in this pit appears to have healed the warriors and preserved them from harm.

In an article on "The Fairy Mythology of Europe in its Relation to Early History,"[62] Mr. A. S. Herbert iden-

---

59   "Testimony of Tradition," p. 68.

60   See "The Picts and Pets" in the Antiquary for May, 1906, p. 172.

61   "The Irish Version of the Historia Britonum of Nennius," edited, with a translation and notes, by James H. Todd, D.D., F.T.C. (Dublin, 1848). The verse quoted is given at p. lxix, additional notes.

62   See the *Nineteenth Century*, February, 1908.

tifies the early dwarf race with Palæolithic man, and states that from such skeletons as have been unearthed "it is believed that they were a people of Mongolian or Turanian origin, short, squat, yellow-skinned, and swarthy."

Professor J. Kollmann, of Basle, speaking of dwarf races, describes "the flat, broad face, with a flat, broad, low nose and large nose roots."[63]

Compare these statements with the description given by Harris in the eighteenth century of the native inhabitants of the northern and eastern coasts of Ireland. "They are," he says, "of a squat sett Stature, have short, broad Faces, thick Lips, hollow Eyes, and Noses cocked up, and seem to be a distinct people from the Western Irish, by whom they are called Clan-galls—*i.e.*, the offspring of the Galls. The curious may carry these observations further. Doubtless a long intercourse and various mixtures of the natives have much worn out these distinctions, of which I think there are yet visible remains."[64]

We have, indeed, had in Ireland from very early times a mingling of various races, but in the North we are in

---

63   See "Ein dolichokephaler Schädel aus dem Dachsenbüel und die Bedeutung der kleinen Menschenrassen für das Abstammungsproblem der Grossen." His words are: "In dem platten, breiten Gesicht sitzt dann eine platte, breite, niedrige Nase, mit breiter Nasenwürzel." He is speaking of the characteristics of the present dwarf races found throughout the world, and quotes the authority of Hagen.

64   Sir James Ware's "Antiquities of Ireland," translated, revised, and improved, with many material additions, by Walter Harris, Esq., vol. ii., chap. ii., p. 17 (Dublin, 1764). The above is taken from one of the additional notes by Harris.

the home of the Irish Picts or Cruithnians, and possibly this description of Harris may indicate that some of the inhabitants in his day bore marks of a dwarfish ancestry. I have already drawn attention to a statement in an old Irish manuscripT[65] that the Luchorpan or wee-bodies, the Fomores and others, were of the race of Ham. Keating also speaks of the Fomorians being sea-rovers of the race of Cam (Ham), who fared from Africa,[66] and states that among the articles of tribute exacted by them from the race of Neimhidh were two-thirds of the children. Unless these were all slaughtered, we have here an intermingling of races, and in the same way it would be quite possible that Finn McCoul might be a tall man, and yet the leader of the small Pechts. The capture of women and children has been a common practice among savage races, and this I believe to be the origin of many fairy-tales, rather than any reference to the abode of the dead. Throughout the "Colloquy of the Ancients," Finn and the Fianna frequently enter the green sidh—the mound where the Tuatha de Danann dwell, and from which the fairies derive their name "fir-sidh." Sometimes they fight as allies of the inmates; frequently they intermarry with them.[67] Throughout this colloquy the dwellers in the sidh possess many magical powers, but they hardly

65 Quoted by Mr. Standish H. O'Grady in "Silva Gadelica" (translation and notes), pp. 563, 564. See Ante p. 32.

66 Keating's "History of Ireland," book i., chap. viii. Translation by P. W. Joyce, LL.D., M.R.I.A.

67 See Cael's "Wooing of Credhe" in "The Colloquy of the Ancients"; "Silva Gadelica," by Standish H. O'Grady, volume with translation and notes, pp. 119-122.

appear as gods of the ancient Irish, and the verse in Fiacc's hymn referring to the worship of the Sidis is not among the stanzas regarded as genuine by Professor Bury.[68]

We see that both in Ireland and Switzerland there are many legends of dwarf races who inhabit underground dwellings. In Switzerland their skeletons have been found. Those discovered by Dr. Nuesch at Schweizersbild, near Schaffhausen, have been minutely described by Dr. J. Kollmann, Professor of Anatomy at Basle.[69] This burial-place dates from the early Neolithic period; in it are found skeletons belonging to men of ordinary height, and in close proximity the graves of dwarfs.

The neighbourhood of Schaffhausen appears to be rich in the remains of early man; several skeletons have been found in the cave of Dachsenbüel, two of them of small men, "such as in Africa would be accounted pygmies."[70] Professor Kollmann mentions several other places in Switzerland where skeletons of dwarfs have been found, as also in the Grotte des Enfants on the Bay of Genoa. He also speaks of dwarf races existing at the present day in Sicily, Sardinia, Sumatra, the Philippine Islands, besides the well-known Veddas of Ceylon, the Andaman Islanders, and the African

---

68   See "Life of St. Patrick," p. 264.

69   See Der Mensch, "Separat-Abzug aus den Denkschriften der Schweiz Naturforschenden Gesellschaft," Band xxxv, 1896.

70   See the paper already referred to, "Ein dolichokephaler Schädel," etc. Professor J. Kollmann's words are: "Die man in Africa wohl zu den Pygmäen zählen wurde."

pygmies. He believes that these small people represent the oldest form of human beings, and that from them the taller races have been evolved.

How long did these primitive people continue to exist in Ireland and in Switzerland? It would be difficult to say. Tradition ascribes to them a strong physique, but even if they could hold their own with the taller races in the Neolithic period, it must have been hard for them to contend with those who used weapons of bronze or iron, and, as we have seen, iron is specially obnoxious to the fairies. The people, however, who built the large number of souterrains dotted over Antrim and Down could not be easily exterminated. Many of them may have been enslaved or gradually absorbed in the rest of the population; others would take refuge in retired spots, such as are still spoken of as "gentle" or haunted by fairies. If I might hazard a conjecture, I should say that both in Ireland and in Switzerland dwarf races had survived far into Christian times, perhaps to a comparatively recent period. The Irish fairy may possibly represent those who refused to accept the teaching of St. Patrick and St. Columbkill, while St. Gall and other Irish monks may have numbered Swiss dwarfs among their converts. Be this as it may, we have certainly in Ulster the tradition of two dwarf races, the small Danes and the Pechts, who are undoubtedly human. We are shown their handiwork, and, primitive as are their underground dwellings, the builders of the souterrains had advanced far beyond the stage when man could only find shelter in the caves provided for him by Nature. How many centuries did he take to learn the lesson? It is a far-reaching question, but here fairy-tales and popular legends are silent. They keep no count of time, although they may bring to us whispers from long-past ages.

FOLKLORE FROM DONEGAL[71]

The stories current among the peasantry are varied, especially in Donegal, where we hear of giants and fairies, of small and tall Finns, of short, stout Firbolgs or Firwolgs, of Danes who made heather ale, and sometimes of Pechts with their large feet.

According to one legend, the fairies were angels who had remained neutral during the great war in heaven. They are sometimes represented as kindly, but often as mischievous. Near Dungiven, in Co. Derry, I was told of a friendly fairy who, dressed as an old woman, came one evening to a cottage where a poor man and his wife lived. She said to the wife that if the stone at the foot of the table were lifted she would find something that would last her all her days. As soon as the visitor was gone, the wife called to her husband to bring a crowbar; they raised the stone, and under it was a crock of gold.

The old man who related this story to me had himself found in a bog a crock covered with a slate. He hoped it might be full of gold, but it only contained bog butter, which he used for greasing cart-wheels.

A carman at Rosapenna told me how the fairies would lead people astray, carrying one man off to Scotland. A girl had her face twisted through their

---

71   Read before the Archæological Section of the Belfast Naturalists' Field Club, February 8, 1911.

influence, and had to go to the priest to be cured. "He was," the man added, "one of the old sort, who could work miracles, of whom there are not many nowadays." Near Finntown a girl had offended the fairies by washing clothes in a "gentle" burn, or stream haunted by the little people. Her eyes were turned to the back of her head. She, too, invoked the aid of a priest, and his blessing restored them to their proper place.

Donegal fairies appear able to adapt themselves to modern conditions. I was told at Finntown they did not interfere with the railway, as they sometimes enjoyed a ride on the top of the train. Although usually only seen in secluded spots, they occasionally visit a fair or market, but are much annoyed if recognized.

In the following story we have an illustration of intercourse between fairies and human beings: An old woman at Glenties was called upon by a strange man to give her aid at the birth of a child. At first she refused, but he urged her, saying it was not far, and in the end she consented. When he brought her to his dwelling she saw a daughter whom she had supposed to be dead, but who was now the wife of the fairy man. The daughter begged her not to let it be known she was her mother, and, giving her a ring, bade her look on it at times and she would know when they could meet. She also added that her husband would certainly offer a reward, but she implored her mother not to accept it, but to ask that the red-haired boy might be given to her. "He will not be willing to part from him," the daughter added; "but if you beg earnestly, he will give him to you in the end."

The mother attended her daughter, and when his child was born the fairy man offered her a rich reward, but she refused, praying only that the red-haired boy might be given to her. At first the father refused, but when she pleaded her loneliness, he granted her request. The daughter was well pleased, told her mother they might meet at the fair on the hill behind Glenties, but warned her that even if she saw the fairy man she must never speak to him. The old woman returned to her home, taking her grandson, the red-haired boy, with her. She kept the ring carefully, and it gave her warning when she would meet her daughter on the hill at Glenties. These interviews were for a long time a great comfort to mother and daughter, but one day, in the joy of her heart, the mother shook hands with and spoke to the fairy man. He turned to her angrily asking how she could see him, and with that he blew upon her eyes, so that she could no longer discern fairies. The precious ring also disappeared, and she never again saw her daughter.

Variants of this story were told to me by an old woman at Portstewart, and by a man whom I met near Lough Salt during the Rosapenna Conference of Field Clubs. In these versions there is no mention of the red-haired boy, nor of the old woman being the mother of the fairy man's wife; she is simply called in to attend to her. When rubbing ointment on the infant, she accidentally draws her hand across one of her eyes and acquires the power of seeing the fairies. Shortly afterwards she meets the fairy man at a market or fair, and inquires for his wife. He is annoyed at being recognized, asks with which eye she sees him, blows upon it, and puts it out.[72]

In another Donegal legend the fairies gain possession of a bride, and would have kept her in captivity had not their plans been frustrated by a mortal. This is the story as told to me near Gweedore, and also at Kincasslagh, a small seaport in the Rosses. Owen Boyle lived with his mother near Kincasslagh, and worked as a carpenter. One Hallow Eve, on his return home, he

---

72   In "Celtic Folklore," vol. i., p. 210 *et seq.*, Sir John Rhys relates a similar story. Here the woman is brought to a place which appears to her to be the finest she has ever seen. When the child is born the father gives her ointment to anoint its eyes, but entreats her not to touch her own with it. Inadvertently she rubs her finger across her eye, and now she sees that the wife is her former maidservant Eilian, and that she lies on a bundle of rushes and withered leaves in a cave. Not long afterwards the woman sees the husband in the market at Carnarvon, and asks for Eilian. He is angry, and, inquiring with which eye she sees him, puts it out with a bulrush.

From Palestine we have another variant of this story. The Rev. J. E. Hanauer, in "Folklore of the Holy Land," pp. 210et seq., tells of a woman at El Welejeh who had spoken unkindly to a frog. The next night, on waking, she found herself in a cave surrounded by strange, angry-looking people; one of these "Jân" reproached her bitterly, saying that the frog was his wife, and threatening her with dire consequences unless a son were born. She assisted at the birth of the child, who was fortunately a boy, and was given a mukhaleh or kohlvessel, and was bidden to rub some of this kohl on the infant's eyes. When she had done this, she rubbed some on one of her own eyes, but before she had time to put any on the other the vessel was angrily taken from her. She was rewarded with onion-leaves, which in the morning turned to gold. Some time afterwards this woman was shopping at El Kuds, when she saw the Jennizeh pilfering from shop to shop. She spoke to her and kissed the baby, but the other answered fiercely, and, poking her finger into the woman's eye, put it out.

found a calf was missing, and went out to look for it. He was told it was behind a stone near the spink or rock of Dunathaid, and when he got there he saw the calf, but it ran away and disappeared through an opening in the rock. Owen was at first afraid to follow, but suddenly he was pushed in, and the door closed behind him. He found himself in a company of fairies, and heard them saying: "This is good whisky from O'Donnel's still. He buried a nine-gallon keg in the bog; it burst, the hoops came off, and the whisky has come to us." One of the fairies gave Owen a glass, saying he might be useful to them that night. They asked if he would be willing to go with them, and, being anxious to get out of the cave, he at once consented. They all mounted on horses, and away they went through Dungloe, across the hills to Dochary, then to Glenties, and through Mount Charles to Ballyshannon, and thence to Connaught. They came to a house where great preparations were being made for a wedding. The fairies told Owen to go in and dance with any girl who asked him. He was much pleased to see that he was now wearing a good suit of clothes, and gladly joined in the dance. After a time there was a cry that the bride would choose a partner, and the partner she chose was Owen Boyle. They danced until the bride fell down in a faint, and the fairies, who had crept in unseen, bore her away. They mounted their horses and took the bride with them, sometimes one carrying her and sometimes another. They had ridden thus for a time when one of the fairies said to Owen: "You have done well for us to-night." "And little I have got for it," was the reply; "not even a turn of carrying the bride." "That you ought to have," said the fairy, and called out to give the bride to Owen. Owen took her, and, urging his horse, outstripped the fairies. They pursued him, but at Bal Cruit Strand he drew with a black knife a circle round himself and the bride, which the fairies could not cross. One of them, however, stretched out a long arm and struck the bride on the face, so that she became deaf and dumb. When the fairies left him, Owen brought the girl to his mother, and in reply to her questions, said he had brought home one to whom all kindness should be shown. They gave her the best seat by the fire; she helped in the housework, but remained speechless.

A year passed, and on Hallow Eve Owen went again to Dunathaid. The door of the cave was open. He entered boldly, and found the fairies enjoying themselves as before. One of them recognized him, and said: "Owen Boyle, you played us a bad trick when you carried off that woman." "And a pretty woman you left with me! She can neither hear nor speak!" "Oh!" said another, "if she had a taste of this bottle, she could do both!" When Owen heard these words he seized the bottle, ran home with it, and, pouring a little into a glass, gave it to the poor girl to drink. Hearing and speech were at once restored. Owen returned the bottle to the fairies, and, before long, he set out for Connaught, taking the girl with him to restore her to her parents. When he arrived, he asked for a night's lodging for himself and his companion. The mother, although she said she had little room, admitted them, and soon Owen saw her looking at the girl. "Why are you gazing at my companion?" he asked. "She is so like a daughter of mine who died a twelvemonth ago." "No," replied Owen; "she did not die; she was carried off by the fairies, and here she is." There was great rejoicing, and before long Owen was married to the girl, the former bridegroom having gone away. He brought her home to Kincasslagh, and not a mile from the village, close to Bal Cruit Strand, may be seen the ring which defended her and Owen from the fairies. It is a very large fairy ring, but why the grass should grow luxuriantly on it tradition does not say.

During the Field Club Conference at Rosapenna a variant of this story was told me by a lad on the heights above Gortnalughoge Bay. Here the man who rode with the fairies was John Friel, from Fanad. They went to Dublin and brought away a young girl from her bed, leaving something behind, which the parents believed to be their dead daughter. Meanwhile the young girl was taken northwards by the fairies. As they drew near to Fanad, John Friel begged to be allowed to carry her, and quickly taking her to his own cottage, kept her there with his mother. The girl was deaf and dumb, but there was no mention of the magic circle or of the blow from the fairy's hand. At the end of the year John Friel, like Owen Boyle, pays another visit to the fairies, overhears their conversation, snatches the bottle, and a few drops from it restore speech and hearing to the girl. He takes her to Dublin. Her parents cannot at first believe that she is truly theirdaughter, but the mother recognizes her by a mark on the shoulder, and the tale ends with great rejoicing.[73]

In these stories we see the relations between fairies and mortals. The fairy man marries a human wife; he appears solicitous for her health, and is willing to pay a high reward to the nurse, but the caution his wife gives to her mother shows her fear of him, and when the latter forgets this warning and speaks to the husband, he effectively stops all intercourse between her and her daughter.

In another story we see that it was the living girl who was carried off, and only a false image left to deceive her parents.[74] It is true that, through the magic of the fairies, she becomes deaf and dumb, but when this is overcome, she returns home safe and sound. The black knife used by Owen Boyle was doubtless an iron knife, that metal being always obnoxious to the fairies.

Stories of children being carried off by fairies are numerous. There was a man lived near Croghan Fort, not far from Lifford, who was short, and had a cataract—or, as the country-people call it, a pearl—on his eye. He was returning home after the birth of his child, when he met the fairies carrying off the infant. They

---

73   In "Guleesh na Guss Dhu," Dr. Douglas Hyde gives us a similar tale from Co. Mayo. See "Beside the Fire," pp. 104-128.

74   In "Folk Tales from Breffny," by B. Hunt, there is a story (pp. 99-103), "The Cutting of the Tree," which tells of how the fairies, when baffled in their endeavour to carry off the mistress of the house, left in the kitchen a wooden image "cut into the living likeness of the woman of the house."

were about to change a benwood into the likeness of a child, saying:

> "*Make it wee, make it short;*
> *Make it like its ain folk;*
> *Put a pearl in its eye;*
> *Make it like its Dadie.*"

Here the man interrupted them, throwing up sand, and exclaiming: "In the name of God, this to youse and mine to me!" They flung his own child at him, but it broke its hinch, or thigh, and was a cripple all its days.

TORMORE, TORY ISLAND.

It is not often that fairies are associated with the spirits of the departed, but in Tory Island and in some other parts of Donegal it is believed that those who are drowned become fairies. In Tory Island I also heard that those who exceeded in whisky met the same fate.

According to the inhabitants of this island, fairies can make themselves large or small; their hair may be red, white, or black; but they dress in black—a very unusual colour for fairies to appear in. It may perhaps be explained by remembering that Tory Island, or Toirinis, was a stronghold of the Fomorians, whom Keating describes as "sea rovers of the race of Cam, who fared from Africa."[75] I need hardly add that "Cam" is an old name for "Ham." I should infer that the fairies of Tory Island represent a dark race.

King Balor, it is true, is not of diminutive stature. I heard much of this chieftain with the eye at the back of his head, which, if uncovered, would kill anyone exposed to its gaze. He knew it had been said in old times that he should die by the hand of his daughter's son, and he determined his daughter should remain childless. He shut her up in Tormore, with twelve ladies to wait on her. Balor had no smith on the island, but at Cloghanealy, on the mainland, there lived a smith who had the finest cow in the world, named Glasgavlen. He kept a boy to watch it, but, notwithstanding this precaution, two of Balor's servants carried off the cow. When the herd-boy saw it was gone, he wept bitterly, for the smith had told him his head would be taken off if he did not bring her back. Suddenly a fairy, Geea Dubh, came out of the rock, and told the boy the cow was in Tory, and if he followed her advice he would get it back. She made a curragh for him, and he crossed over to Tory, but he did not get the cow. The tale now becomes confused. We hear of twelve children, and how Balor ordered them all to be drowned, but his

---

75   See *ante*, p. 56.

daughter's son was saved. The fairy told the herd-boy that, if the child were taken care of, it would grow up like a crop which, when put into the earth one day, sprouts up the next.

The boy took service under Balor, and the child was sent to the ladies, who brought him up for three years. At the end of that time the herd boy took him to the mainland, where he grew up a strong youth, and worked for the smith. On one occasion Balor sent messengers across to the mainland, but the lad attacked them and cut out their tongues. The maimed messengers returned to Tory, and when Balor saw them he knew that he who had done this deed was the dreaded grandson. He set out to kill him; but when the youth saw Balor approaching the forge, he drew the poker from the fire and thrust it into the eye at the back of the King's head.

The wounded Balor called to his grandson to come to him, and he would leave him everything. The youth was wise; he did not go too near Balor, but followed him from Falcarragh to Gweedore. "Are you near me?" was the question put by the King as he walked along, water streaming from his wounded eye; and this water formed the biggest lough in the world, three times as deep as Lough Foyle.

I have given this story as it was told to me by an elderly man in a cottage on Tory Island.

A version of it is related by the late Most Rev. Dr. MacDevitt in the "Donegal Highlands." It is referred to by Mr. Stephen Gwynn, M.P., in "Highways and

Byways in Donegal and Antrim," and a very full narrative is given by Dr. O'Donovan in a note in his edition of the "Annals of the Four Masters."[76] Dr. O'Donovan states that he had the story from Shane O'Dugan, whose ancestor is said to have been living in Tory in the time of St. Columbkille. Here we read of the stratagem by which Balor, assuming the shape of a red-haired little boy, carried off the famous cow Glasgavlen from the chieftain MacKineely, and it is not the herdboy, but the chieftain himself, who is wafted across to Tory Island and introduced to Balor's daughter. Three sons are born; Balor orders them all to be drowned, but the eldest is saved by the friendly banshee and taken to his father, who places him in fosterage under his brother, the great smith Gavida. After a time MacKineely falls a victim to the vengeance of Balor, and is beheaded on the stone Clough-an-neely, where the marks of his blood may still be seen.

Balor now deems himself secure. He often visits the forge of Gavida, and one day, when there, boasts of his conquest of MacKineely. No sooner has he uttered the proud words than the young smith seizes a glowing rod from the furnace and thrusts it through Balor's basilisk eye so far that it comes out at the other side of his head.

It will be noted that in this version Balor's death is instantaneous; nothing is said about the deep lough formed by the water from his eye.

According to O'Flaherty's "Ogygia," Balor was killed at the second battle of Moyture "by a stone

---

76   See *ante*.

thrown at him by his grandson by his daughter from a machine called Tabhall (which some assert to be a sling)."[77]

If Balor is the grim hero of Tory Island, on the mainland we hear much of Finn McCoul. I was informed that he had an eye at the back of his head, and was so tall his feet came out at the door of his house. How large the house was, tradition does not say. The island of Carrickfinn opposite to Bunbeg is said to have been a favourite hunting-ground of Finn McCoul. When crossing over to this island, I was told by the boatman that the Danes were stout, small, and red-haired, and that they lived in the caves. The Finns, he said, were even smaller, dark yellow people.

Near Loughros Bay I saw the Cashel na Fian, but whether it was built by tall or small Finns I do not know. Part of the wall was standing, built in the usual fashion with stones without mortar.

This cashel was on a height, and near it I was shown some old fields, the ridges farther apart than those of the present day, and I was told they might be the fields of those who built the cashel, or perhaps of the Firbolgs. The old man who acted as my guide softened the *b* in the Irish manner, and spoke of those people as the Firwolgs; he said they were short and stout, and cultivated the lands near the sea.

To the Danes are ascribed the kitchen-middens on Rosguill, and the lad I met above Gortnalughoge Bay, told me they lived and had their houses on the water,

---

77 "Ogygia," part iii., chap. xii.

I should infer after the fashion of the lake-dwellers. He could not tell me the height of these Danes, but those who built the forts and cashels have often been described to me as short and red-haired. As I have stated on former occasions, I should be inclined to identify these short Danes with the Tuatha de Danann. I visited one of their cashels above Dungiven, under which there is a souterrain, and I also went to one on a hill above Downey's pier at Rosapenna. I believe it is the Downey's Fort marked on the Ordnance Survey map. It appeared to be regarded as an uncanny spot; treasure is said to be hidden under it, and I had a difficulty in getting anyone to take me to it. A little girl, however, acted as guide, and a young farmer, who had at first refused, joined me on the top. I took some very rough measurements of this cashel. From the outer circumference it was about 60 by 60 feet; the walls had fallen inwards, so it was impossible to say how thick they had been originally, but the space free from stones in the centre measured about 25 by 25 feet.

The young farmer told me of some rocks at a place he called Dooey, on which crosses were inscribed. I believe that near Mevagh, in addition to the spiral markings, which were visited by many members of the Conference, there is another rock on which crosses are also inscribed.

Firbolgs, Danes, Finns, and Pechts, of whom I have spoken on former occasions, are all strictly human; and if the fairy has been more spiritualized, I think, in many of the traditions, we may see how closely he is allied to ancient and modern pygmies.

Fairies intermarry freely with the human race; they are not exempt from death, and sometimes come to a violent end. At Kincasslagh a graphic story was told me by an old woman of how two banshees attacked a man when he was crossing the "banks" at Mullaghderg. His faithful dog had been chained at home, but, knowing the danger, escaped, saved his master, and killed one of the banshees. Her body was found next morning in the sand: she had wonderful eyes, small legs, and very large feet. I may mention that large feet are character-istic of the Pechts.

It is true that those who are drowned may become fairies, but if a fisherman be missing, who shall say whether he lies at the bottom of the ocean or has been carried captive to a lonely cave. In later times, when the fairies were associated with fallen angels, one who had not received the last rites of the Church might naturally be supposed to become a fairy.

In the tales of the giants we are brought face to face with beings of great strength, but in a low stage of civili-zation. Balor, we have seen, had no smith on Tory Island, and in a story of the fight between the giant Fargowan and a wild boar, his sister Finglas goes to his assistance with her apron filled with stones. Misled by the echo, she jumps backwards and forwards across Lough Finn until at last her long hair becomes entangled and she is drowned. It is believed that her coffin was found when the railway was being made; the boards were 14 feet long. Sometimes the works of Nature are ascribed to the giants; we have all heard of Finn McCoul as the artificer of the Giant's Causeway, and near Glenties I was shown perched blocks, which had been thrown by the giants. On the other hand, these giants, with all their magic, are often very human; perhaps we are listening to the tales of a small race, who exaggerated the feats of their large but savage neighbours. Writing in 1860, J. F. Campbell, in his introduction to the "Tales of the West Highlands," says: "Probably, as it seems to me, giants are simply the nearest savage race at war with the race who tell the tales. If they performed impossible feats of strength, they did no more than Rob Roy, whose putting-stone is now shown to Saxon tourists ... in the shape of a boulder of many tons."[78] Turning to fairies, the same writer says: "I believe there was once a small race of people in these islands, who are remembered as fairies.... They are always represented as living in green mounds. They pop up their heads when disturbed by people treading on their houses. They steal children. They seem to live on familiar terms with the people about them when they treat them well, to punish them when they ill-treat them.... There are such people now. A Lapp is such a man; he is a little flesh-eating mortal, having control over the beasts, and living in a green mound, when he is not living in a tent or sleeping out of doors, wrapped in his deerskin shirt."[79]

Since these words were written, our knowledge of dwarf races has been greatly increased; their skeletons have been found in Switzerland and other parts of

78   Pp. xcix, c.
79   Pp. c, ci.

Europe. We are all familiar with the pygmies of Central Africa, and the members of this Club will remember the interesting photographs of them shown by Sir Harry Johnston. Besides the Andamnan Islanders, we have dwarf races in various parts of Asia, and doubtless we have all read with interest the account of the New Guinea dwarfs, sent by the members of the British Expedition, who are investigating that Island under many difficulties.

Dr. Eric Marshall describes these pygmies as "averaging four feet six inches to four feet eight inches in height, wild, shy, treacherous little devils; these little men wander over the heavy jungle-clad hills, subsisting on roots and jungle produce, hunting the wallaby, pig, and cassowary, and fishing in the mountain torrents.... The only metal tool they possessed was a small, wedge-shaped piece of iron, one inch by two inches, inserted into a wooden handle, and answering the purpose of an axe, and with this the whole twenty-acre clearing had been made. None but those who have worked and toiled in this dense jungle can really appreciate the perseverance and patience necessary to accomplish this, for many of the trees are from twelve to fifteen feet in circumference."[80]

Throughout Donegal we find many traces of the primitive belief that men or women can change themselves into animals. At Rosapenna I was told of a hare

---

80   See *Morning Post*, December 28, 1910. In his work, "Pygmies and Papuans," which gives the results of this expedition, Mr. A. F. R. Wollaston also describes these pygmies (see especially pp. 159-161).

standing on its hind-legs like an old woman and sucking a cow, the inference being plainly that the witch had transformed herself into a hare. I heard similar stories at Glenties. Here I was told of a man who killed a young seal, but was startled when the mother, weeping, cried out in Irish: "My child, my child!" Never again did he kill a seal.

A story illustrating the same belief is told by John Sweeney, an inspector of National Schools, who wrote about forty years ago a series of letters describing Donegal and its inhabitants.[81] In his account of Arranmore he says: "Until lately the islanders could not be induced to attack a seal, they being strongly under the impression that these animals were human beings metamorphosed by the power of their own witchcraft. In confirmation of this notion, they used to repeat the story of one Rodgers of their island, who, being alone in his skiff fishing, was overtaken by a storm, and driven on the shore of the Scotch Highlands. Having landed, he approached a house which was close to the beach, and on entering it was accosted by name. Expressing his surprise at finding himself known in a strange country, and by one whom he had never seen, the old man who addressed him bared his head, and, pointing to a scar on his skull, reminded Rodgers of an encounter he had with a seal in one of the caves of

---

81   I was shown a MS. copy of some of these letters by a relative of the writer at Burtonport. I believe they were written for a newspaper, and were afterwards republished in "The Derry People," under the title "The Rosses Thirty Years Ago." They contain much interesting information in regard to the traditions current among the peasantry.

Arranmore. 'I was,' he said, 'that seal, and this is the mark of the wound you inflicted on me. I do not blame you, however, for you were not aware of what you were doing.'"

I fear I have lingered too long over these old-world stories. To me they point to a far-distant past, when Ulster was covered with forests, in which the red deer and perhaps the Irish elk roamed, and inhabited by rude tribes, some of them of dwarfish stature, others tall; but these giants were apparently even less civilized than their smaller neighbours. Wars were frequent; the giant could hurl the unwieldy mass of stone, and the dwarfish man could send his arrow tipped with flint. Even more common was the stealthy raid, when women and children were carried off to the gloomy souterrain. How long did these rude tribes survive? It would be difficult to say; possibly until after the days of St. Patrick and St. Columkill.

I will not, however, indulge in a fancy sketch. The pressing need is not to interpret but to collect these old tales. The antiquary of the future, with fuller knowledge at his command, may be better able to decipher them; but if they are allowed to perish, one link with the past will be irretrievably lost.

GIANTS AND DWARFS [82]

The population of Ulster is derived from many sources, and in its folklore we shall find traces of various tribes and people. I shall begin with a tale which may have been brought by English settlers.

In "Folklore as an Historical Science" Sir G. Laurence Gomme has given several variants of the story of the Pedlar of Swaffham and London Bridge. Most of these come from England, Scotland, and Wales, but among them there are also a Breton and a Norse version. I have found a local variant in Donegal. An elderly woman told me that at Kinnagoe a "toon" or small hamlet about three miles from Buncrana, there lived a man whose name, she believed, was Doherty. He dreamt one night that on London Bridge he should hear of a treasure. He set out at once for London, and when he came there walked up and down the bridge until he was wearied. At last a man accosted him and asked him why he loitered there. In reply, Doherty told his dream, upon which the other said: "Ah, man! Do you believe in drames? Why, I dreamt the other night that at a place called Kinnagoe a pot of gold is buried. Would I go to look for it? I might loss my time if I paid attention to drames." "That's true," answered Doherty, who now hurried home, found the pot of gold, bought houses and land, and became a wealthy man.

Whether this story embodies an earlier Irish legend I do not know, but I should say that the mention of

---

82 Reprinted from the *Antiquary*, August, 1913.

London Bridge points to its having been brought over by English settlers. Sir G. L. Gomme tells us that "the earliest version of this legend is quoted from the manuscripts of Sir Roger Twysden, who obtained it from Sir William Dugdale, of Blyth Hall, in Warwickshire, in a letter dated January 29, 1652-53. Sir William says of it that 'it was the tradition of the inhabitants, as it was told me there.'"

May not some of the planters brought over by the Irish Society have carried this legend from their English home, giving it in the name Kinnagoe a local habitation?

Most of our folklore comes, however, from a very early period. Our Irish fairy, although regarded as a fallen angel, is not the medieval elf, who could sip honey from a flower, but a small old man or woman with magical powers, swift to revenge an injury, but often a kindly neighbour. No story is told more frequently than that of the old fairy woman who borrows a "noggin" of meal, repays it honestly, and rewards the peasant woman by saying that her kist will never be empty, generally adding the condition as long as the secret is kept. The woman usually observes the condition until her husband becomes too inquisitive. When she reveals the secret the kist is empty.

Another widespread tale is that of the fairy woman who comes to the peasant's cottage, sometimes to beg that water may not be thrown out at the door, as it comes down her chimney and puts out the fire; sometimes to ask, for a similar reason, that the "byre," or cowhouse, may be removed to another site. In some tales it is a fairy man who makes the request. If it is refused, punishment follows in sickness among the cattle; if complied with, the cows flourish and give an extra supply of milk. In one instance the "wee folk" provided money to pay a mason to build the new cowhouse. We may smile, and ask how the position of the cowhouse could affect the homes of the fairies; but if these small people lived in the souterrains, as tradition alleges, we may even at the present day find these artificial caves under inhabited houses. At a large farmhouse on the border of Counties Antrim and Londonderry I was told one ran under the kitchen. At another farm near Castlerock, Co. Londonderry, the owner opened a trapdoor in his yard, and allowed me to look down into a souterrain. At Finvoy, Co. Antrim, I was shown one of these caves over which a cottage formerly stood. A souterrain also runs under the Glebe House at Donaghmore, Co. Down. The following extract is from a work[83] in preparation, by the Rev. Dr. Cowan, Rector of the parish, who, in describing this souterrain, writes: "The lintel to the main entrance is the large stone which forms the base of the old Celtic cross, which stands a few yards south of the church. Underneath the cross is the central chamber, which is sixty-two feet long, three feet wide and upwards of four feet high, with branches in the form of transepts about thirty feet in length. From these, again, several sections extend ... one due north terminating at the

---

83 "An Ancient Irish Parish, Past and Present."

Glebe House (a distance of two hundred yards) under-neath the study, where, according to tradition, some rich old vicar in past times fashioned the extreme end into the dimensions of a wine-cellar."

According to another tradition—an older one, no doubt—this chamber under the study was the dressing-room of the small Danes, who after their toilet proceeded through the underground passages to church. They had to pass through many little doors, down stairs, through parlours, until they came to the great chamber under the cross where the minister held forth. I shall not attempt to guess to what old faith this minister or priest belonged, or what were the rites he celebrated; but the stairs probably represent the descent from one chamber to another, and the little doors the bridges found in some souterrains, and, I believe, at Donaghmore, where one stone juts out from the floor, and a little farther on another comes down from the roof, leaving only a narrow passage, so that one must creep over and under these bridges to get to the end of the cave.

The Danes are regarded by the country people as distinctly human, and yet there is much in them that reminds us of the fairies; indeed, I was told by two old men—one in Co. Antrim, and the other in Co. Derry—that they and the wee-folk are much the same. In a former paper[84] I referred to the difference in dress ascribed to the fairies in various parts of the country. I am inclined to believe that this indicates a variety

---

84   See *Ulster Fairies*, Danes, and Pechts, p. 27.

of tribes among the aboriginal inhabitants. In the fairies who dress in green may we not have a tradition of people who stained themselves with woad or some other plant? These fairies are chiefly heard of in North-East Antrim. In some parts of that county they are said to wear tartan, but in other parts of Ulster the fairies are usually, although not universally, described as dressing in red. Do these represent a people who dyed themselves with red ochre, or who simply went naked? In Tory Island I was told the fairies dressed in black; and Keating informs us that the Fomorians, who had their headquarters at Toirinis, or Tory Island, were "sea-rovers of the race of Cam, who fared from Africa."[85]

Stories of the fairies or wee-folk are to be found everywhere in Ulster, and the Danes are also universally known; but one hears of the Pechts, chiefly in the north-east of Antrim, where the Grogach is also known. The following story was told to me in Glenariff, Co. Antrim:

A Grogach herded the cattle of a farmer, and drove them home in the evening. He was about the size of a child, and was naked. A fire was left burning at night so that he might warm himself, and after a time the daughter of the house made him a shirt. When the Grogach saw this he thought it was a "billet" for him to go, and, crying bitterly, he took his departure, and left the shirt behind him. As I pointed out on a former

---

85 Keating, "History of Ireland," book i., chap. viii. (translation by P. W. Joyce, LL.D., M.R.I.A.). See *ante*, p. 56.

occasion,[86] in many respects the Grogach resembles the Swiss dwarf. The likeness to the Brownie is also very marked. At Ballycastle I was told the Grogach was a hairy man about four feet in height, who could bear heat or cold without clothing.

Patrick Kennedy has described a Gruagach as a giant, and states that the word "Gruagach" has for root *gruach*—"hair," giants and magicians being"furnished with a large provision of that appendage."[87] This Gruagach was closely related to the fairies, and, indeed, we shall find later in a Donegal story a giant ogress spoken of as a fairy woman. In Scotland, as well as in the South of Ireland, the name is Gruagach, but in Antrim I heard it pronounced "Grogach." I was also told near Cushendall that the Danes were hairy people.

One does not hear so much about giants in An trim as in Donegal, but in Glenariff I was told of four, one of whom lifted a rock at Ballycastle and threw it across the sea to Rathlin—a distance of five or six miles. Great as this feat was, a still greater was reported to me near Armoy,[88] where I was shown a valley, and was told the earth had been scooped out and thrown into the sea, where it formed the Island of Rathlin.

The grave of the giant Gig-na-Gog is to be seen

---

86   See *Traditions of Dwarf Races in Ireland and in Switzerland,* pp. 50-52.

87   "Legendary Fictions of the Irish Celts," second edition, p. 123 note.

88   A village about six miles from Ballycastle, where there is a round tower.

some miles from Portrush on the road to Beardiville.[89] I could not, however, hear anything of Gig-na-Gog, except that he was a giant.

In the stories of giants we no doubt often have traditions of a tall race, who are sometimes represented as of inferior mental capacity. At other times we appear to be listening to an early interpretation of the works of Nature. The Donegal peasant at the present day believes that the perched block on the side of the hill has been thrown by the arm of a giant. In the compact columns of the Giant's Causeway and of Fingal's Cave at Staffa primitive man saw a work of great skill and ingenuity, which he attributed to a giant artificer; and Finn McCoul is credited with having made a stupendous mole, uniting Scotland and Ireland. This Finn McCoul has many aspects. He does not show to much advantage in the following legend, which I heard on the banks of Lough Salt in Donegal: Finn was a giant but there was a bigger giant named Goll, who came to fight Finn, and Finn was afraid. His wife bade him creep into the cradle, and she would give an answer to Goll. When the latter appeared, he asked where was Finn. The wife replied he was out, and she was alone with the baby in the cradle. Goll looked at the child, and thought, if that is the size of Finn's infant, what must Finn himself be? and without more ado he turned and took his departure.[90] This Finn had an eye at the

---

89 It is referred to in the "Guide to Belfast and the Adjacent Counties," by the Belfast Naturalists' Field Club, 1874, pp. 205, 206; also by Borlase in "Dolmens of Ireland," vol. i., p. 371.

90 A similar tale, but with more details, is related of Finn by William

back of his head, and was so tall his feet came out at the door of his house. We are not told, however, what was the size of the house.

VALLEY NEAR ARMOY, WHENCE, ACCORDING TO
LEGEND, EARTH WAS TAKEN TO FORM RATHLIN.

In this tale Finn shows little courage, but as a rule he is represented as a noted hero. I was told a long story at Glenties in Donegal of the three sons Finn had by the Queen of Italy. He had seen her bathing in Ireland, and he stole her clothes, so she had to stay until she could get them back. After a time she found them, and returned to her own country, where she gave birth to

---

Carleton. It was first published in Chambers' Edinburgh Journal in January, 1841, with the title, "A Legend of Knockmary," and was reprinted in Carleton's collected works under the title "A Legend of Knockmany." It is given by Mr. W. B. Yeats in his "Irish Fairy and Folk Tales." In Carleton's tale Finn's opponent is not Goll, but Cuchullin. In the notes first published in Chambers' Journal reference is, however, made to Scotch legends about Finn McCoul and Gaul, the son of Morni, whom I take to be the same as Goll. A version of the story is also given by Patrick Kennedy in "Legendary Fictions of the Irish Celts," under the title "Fann MacCuil and the Scotch Giant," pp. 179-181. This Scotch giant is named Far Rua, and the fort to which he journeys is in the bog of Allen.

three sons—Dubh, Kian, and Glasmait. When they were fourteen years of age the King of Italy sent them away that they might go to their father Finn.

They arrived in Ireland, and when Finn saw them he said: "If those three be the sons of a King, they will come straight on; if not, they will ask their way." The lads came straight on, knelt before Finn, and claimed him as their father. He asked them who was their mother, and when they said the Queen of Italy, Finn remembered the stolen clothes, and received them as his sons.

One day the followers of Finn could not find his dividing knife, and Dubh determined to go in search of it. He put a stick in the fire, and said he would be back before the third of it was burnt out. He followed tracks, and came to a house where there was a great feast. He sat down among the men, and saw they were cutting with Finn's knife. It was passed from one to another until it came to Dubh, who, holding it in his hand, sprang up and carried it off.

When Dubh got home he wakened Kian and said: "My third of the stick is burnt, and now do you see what you can do." Kian followed the tracks, and got to the same place. He found the men drinking out of a horn. One called for whisky, another for wine, and whatever was asked, the horn gave. Kian heard them say it was Finn's horn, and that his knife had been carried off the previous night. Kian waited, and when the horn came he grasped it tightly and ran off home, where he found his third of the stick was burnt. He waked Glasmait, and told him two-thirds of the night had passed, and it was now his turn to go out. Glasmait followed the same tracks, but when he came to the house blood was flowing from the door, and, looking in, he saw the place full of corpses. One man only remained alive. He told Glasmait how they had all been drinking when someone ran off with Finn McCoul's horn. "One man blamed another," he said; "they quarrelled and fought until everyone was killed except myself. Now I beseech you throw the ditch[91] upon me and bury me. I do not wish to be devoured by the fairy woman, who will soon be here. She is an awful size, and upon her back is bound Finn McCoul's sword of light,[92] which gives to its possessor the strength of a hundred men." The man gave Glasmait some hints to aid him in the coming fight, and added: "Now I have told you all, bury me quick."

Glasmait threw the ditch upon him, and hid himself in a corner. The Banmore, or large woman, now came in, and began her horrible repast. She chose the fat men; three times she lifted Glasmait, but rejected him as too young and lean. At last she lay down to sleep. Glasmait followed the advice he had received. He touched her foot, but jumped aside to avoid the kick. He touched her hand, but jumped aside to avoid her slap. When she was again asleep, he drew his sword and cut the cords which bound the sword of light to her back, and seized upon it. She roused herself, and for two hours

91 In Ireland "ditch" is used for an earth fence.

92 Claive Solus was the name given to it by the old woman, who narrated the story, and she translated it "sword of light."

they fought, until in the end Glasmait ripped open her body, when, behold, three red-haired boys sprang out and attacked him. He slew two of them, but the third escaped. Glasmait returned home with the sword of light, and found his third of the stick burnt.

The three sons now presented their father with the dividing knife, the drinking horn, and the sword of light, and there was great rejoicing that these had been recovered.

Some time after this a red-haired boy appeared, and begged to be taken into Finn's service for a twelve-month, saying he could kill birds and do any kind of work. When asked what wages he looked for, he replied that he hoped when he died, Finn and his men would put his body in a cart, which would come for it, and bury him where the cart stopped.

The red-haired boy worked well, but at the end of the year he suddenly died. A cart drawn by a horse appeared, and Finn and his men tried to place the body in it; but it could not be moved until the horse wheeled round and did the work itself, starting immediately afterwards with its load. Finn and his men followed, but a great mist came on, so that they could not see clearly. At last they arrived at an old, black castle standing in a glen. Here they found the table laid, and sat down to eat, but before long the red-haired boy appeared alive, and cried vengeance upon Finn and his sons. The men tried to draw their swords, but found them fastened to the ground, and the red-haired boy cut off fifty heads.

Now, however, the great Manannan appeared. He bade the red-haired boy drop his sword, or he would give him a slap that would turn his face to the back of his head. He also bade him replace the heads on the fifty men. The red-haired boy had to submit, and after that he troubled Finn no more. Manannan dispelled the mist, and brought Finn and his men back to their own home, where they feasted for three days and three nights.

This somewhat gruesome story contains several points of interest. The stealing of the clothes is an incident which occurs with slight variations in many folk-tales. In "The Stolen Veil"[93] Musäus tells us how the damsel of fairy lineage was detained when her veil was carried off, and it was only after she had recovered it that she was able, in the guise of a swan, to return to her home.

We have read, too, of how the Shetlander captured the sealskin of the Finn woman, without which she could not return as a seal to her husband.[94] It should also be noted that the fairy ogress is a large woman, apparently a giantess, while her three sons have the red hair so often associated with the fairies. At the end of the tale Finn and his men are saved by Manannan, the

---

93 See J. K. A. Musäus, "Volksmährchen der Deutschen," edited by J. L. Klee (Leipzig, 1842); "Der geraubte Schleier," pp. 371-429.

94 See "The Testimony of Tradition" (London, 1890, pp. 1-25), by Mr. David MacRitchie, F.S.A.Scot.; also by the same author, "The Aberdeen Kayak and its Congeners." Proceedings of the Society of Antiquaries of Scotland, vol. xlvi. (1911-12), pp. 213-241. Mr. MacRitchie believes that the magic sealskin was a Kayak.

Celtic god of the sea, who has given his name to the Isle of Man. In Balor of Tory Island the great Fomorian chief, we have another giant, with an eye at the back of his head, which dealt destruction to all who encountered its gaze. I was told in Tory Island that when Balor was mortally wounded water fell so copiously from his eye that it formed the biggest lough in the world, deeper even than Lough Foyle.[95]

These giants belonged to an olden time and a very primitive race. They have passed away, and are no longer like the fairies—objects of fear or awe.

The fairies, being believed to be fallen angels, are especially dreaded on Hallow Eve night. In some places oatmeal and salt are put on the heads of the children to protect them from harm. I first heard of this custom in the valley of the Roe, where there are a large number of forts said to be inhabited by the fairies. The neighbourhood of Dungiven on that river is rich in antiquities. I was told there was a souterrain under the Cashel or "White Fort," said to have been built by the Danes. There is another under Carnanban Fort, and not far from this there are the stone circles at Aghlish. An old woman of ninety-six showed them to me, and said it was a very gentle[96] place, and it would not be safe to take away one of the stones.

---

95   See *ante.*

96   Fairy-haunted.

FLINT SPEARHEAD AND BASALT AXES FOUND UNDER FORT IN LENAGH TOWNLAND.

Here we have an instance of the strong belief that to interfere in any way with stone, tree, or fort, belonging to the fairies is certain to bring disaster. About sixty-five years ago, when the railway was being made between Belfast and Ballymena, an old fort with fairy bushes in the townland of Lenagh stood on the intended track, and had to be removed. The men working on the line were most unwilling to meddle with either fort or bushes. One, however, braver than the rest began to cut down a thorn, when he met with an accident which strengthened the others in their refusal. In the end the fort had to be blown up, I believe by the officials of the railway, and underneath it a very fine spearhead and other implements were found.[97]

A fort near Glasdrumman, Co. Down, was demol-

---

97   This spearhead is in the possession of Mr. Robert Bell, a member of the Belfast Naturalists' Field Club, from whom I heard this narrative.

ished by the owner, but the country-people noted that the man who struck the first blow was injured and died soon afterwards, while the owner himself became a permanent invalid. A woman living near this fort related that in the evening after the work was begun she heard an awful screech from the fort; presumably the fairies were leaving their home.

A curious story was told me by an old woman in the Cottage Hospital at Cushendall. A man at Glenravel named M'Combridge went out one evening to look for his heifer, but could not find it. He saw a great house in one of his fields, where no house had been before, and, wondering much at this, he went in. An old woman sat by the fire, and soon two men came in leading the heifer. They killed it with a blow on the head and put it into a pot. M'Combridge was too much afraid to make any objection; he rose, however, to leave the house, but the old woman said: "Wait; you must have some of the broth of your own heifer." Three times she made him partake of the broth, and he was then unable to leave the house. She put him to bed, and the man gave birth to a son. He fell asleep, but was wakened by something touching his ear, and found himself on the grass near his home, and the heifer close to his ear.

This fantastic story no doubt represents a dream, but does it contain a reminiscence of the couvade, where, after the birth of the child, the father goes to bed? Sir E. B. Tylor, in the "Early History of Mankind," has shown how widespread this custom was both in the Old and the New World.

In these stories, drawn from various parts of Ulster, we seem to hear echoes of a very distant past. The giants often appear as savages of low intelligence. In the fairies, I think, we may plainly see a tradition of a dwarf race, although it is true that the country-people do not regard them as human beings; indeed, I was told in Co. Tyrone that when the fairies were annoying a man he threw his handkerchief at them, and asked if among them all they could show one drop of blood. This, being spirits, they could not do. In the Grogach the human element is more pronounced, and both Danes and Pechts are usually regarded as men and women like ourselves, although of smaller stature. It will thus be seen that in Ulster we have traditions of giants, fairies, Grogachs, Danes, and Pechts; and in Donegal I was also told of a small race of yellow Finns. Can we identify any of these with the prehistoric races of the British Isles and of Europe?

It has been held by many that the relics of Palæolithic man do not occur in Ireland, but the Rev. Frederick Smith has found his implements, some of them glaciated, at Killiney;[98] and Mr. Lewis Abbott, who has made the implements of early man a special study, believes that Palæolithic man lived and worked in Ireland. In a letter to me he states that this opinion is based on material in his possession. "I have," he writes, "the Irish collection of my old friend, the late Professor Rupert Jones; in this there are many immensely metamorphosed, deeply iron-stained (and the iron, again, in

98   "The Stone Age in North Britain and Ireland," by the Rev. Frederick Smith, Appendix, p. 396.

turn further altered), implements of Palæolithic types....
They are usually very lustrous or highly 'patinated,' as
it is called." In his recent paper, "On the Classification
of the British Stone Age Industries,"[99] in describing the
club studs, Mr. Abbott writes: "I have found very fine
examples in the Cromer Forest bed, and under and in
various glacial deposits in England and Ireland." How
long Palæolithic man survived in Ireland it would be
difficult to say, but in such characters as the fairy ogress
we are brought face to face with a very low form of
savagery. It will be noted that her sons are red-haired.
Now, I have often found red hair ascribed to fairies and
Danes, but not to Pechts. This persistent tradition has
led me to ask whether red was the colour of the hair in
some early races of mankind. The following passage
in Dr. Beddoe's Huxley Lecture[100] favours an affirma-
tive answer: "There are, of course, facts, or reported
facts, which would lead one to suspect that red was the
original hair colour of man in Europe—at least, when
living in primitive or natural conditions with much
exposure, and that the development of brown pigment
came later, with subjection to heat and malaria, and
other influences connected with what we call 'civilisation.'"

We have seen that the implements of early man are
found in spots sacred to the fairies. The Rev. Gath
Whitley considers the Piskey dwarfs the earliest

---

99   See *Journal of the Royal Anthropological Institute*, vol. xli.,
      1911, p. 462.

100   "Colour and Race," delivered before the Anthropological
      Institute of Great Britain and Ireland, October 31, 1905.

Neolithic inhabitants of Cornwall, and describes them as a small race who hunted the elk and the deer, and perhaps, like the Bushmen, danced and sang to the light of the moon.[101] Our traditional Irish fairies bear a strong resemblance to these Piskey dwarfs of Cornwall, and also to the Welsh fairies of whom Sir John Rhys writes that when fairyland is cleared of its glamour there seems to be disclosed "a swarthy population of short, stumpy men, occupying the most inaccessible districts of our country.... They probably fished and hunted and kept domestic animals, including, perhaps, the pig, but they depended largely on what they could steal at night or in misty weather. Their thieving, however, was not resented, as their visits were believed to bring luck and prosperity."[102] This description might apply to our Ulster fairies, who in many of the stories appear as a very primitive people. In some of the tales, however, the fairies are represented in a higher state of civilisation. They can spin and weave; they inhabit underground but well-built houses, and in the Irish records they are closely associated with the Tuatha de Danann.

I believe these Tuatha de Danann are the small Danes, who, according to tradition, built the raths and souterrains. The late Mr. John Gray[103] would ascribe a Mongoloid origin to them. In a letter written to me shortly before his death he stated his belief that the

---

101   "Footprints of Vanished Races in Cornwall," by the Rev. D. Gath Whitley, published in the *Journal of the Royal Institution of Cornwall*, 1903, vol. xv., part ii., p. 283.

102   "Celtic Folklore," vol. ii., chap. xii., pp. 668, 669.

103   Treasurer to the Anthropological Institute.

Danes and Pechts "were of the same race, and were identical with a short, round-headed race which migrated into the British Isles about 2,000 B.C. at the beginning of the Bronze Age.... The stature of these primitive Danes and Pechts was five feet three inches, and they must have looked very small men to the later Teutonic invaders of an average stature of five feet eight and a half inches."

In his papers, "Who built the British Stone Circles?"[104] and "The Origin of the Devonian Race,"[105] Mr. Gray has fully described this round-headed race, who buried in short cists, and whom he believes to have been a colony from Asia Minor of Akkadians, Sumerians, or Hittites, who migrated to England by sea in order to work the Cornish tin-mines and the Welsh copper-mines.

For a fuller exposition of these views I must refer the reader to Mr. Gray's very interesting articles.

In regard to the Tuatha de Danann, according to Keating,[106] they came from Greece by way of Scandinavia. This might lead us to infer a northern origin, or, at least, that they had taken a different route from those who came by the Mediterranean to the West of Europe. They appear to have known the use of metals and to have ploughed the land.

Dr. O'Donovan, in writing of these Tuatha de

---

104   Read before Section H of the British Association at the Dublin Meeting, September, 1908, published in Nature, December 24, 1908, pp. 236-238.

105   Published in *London Devonian Year-Book*, 1910.

106   "History of Ireland," book i., chap. x.

Danann, says: "From the many monuments ascribed to this colony by tradition and in ancient Irish historical tales, it is quite evident that they were a real people, and from their having been considered gods and magicians by the Gaedhil or Scoti who subdued them, it may be inferred that they were skilled in arts which the latter did not understand." Referring to the colloquy between St. Patrick and Caoilte MacRonain, Dr. O'Donovan says that it appears from this ancient Irish text that "there were very many places in Ireland where the Tuatha de Dananns were then supposed to live as sprites or fairies." He adds: "The inference naturally to be drawn from these stories is that the Tuatha de Dananns lingered in the country for many centuries after their subjugation by the Gaedhil, and that they lived in retired situations, which induced others to regard them as magicians."[107]

What is here averred of the Tuatha de Danann may be true of other primitive races who may have survived long in Ireland. It is difficult to exterminate a people, and they could not be driven farther west.

It appears to me that in the traditions of the Ulster peasantry we see indications of a tall, savage people, and of various races of small men. Some were in all probability veritable dwarfs, like those whose skeletons have been found in Switzerland, near Schaffhausen. Others may have been of the stature of the round-headed race described by Mr. John Gray, but in tradition they all—fairy, Grogach, Pecht, and Dane—appear as little

107   See "Annals of the Four Masters," vol. i., note at p. 24.

people. In these tales we have not a clear outline—the picture is often blurred—but as we see the red-haired Danes carrying earth in their aprons to build the forts, the Pechts handing from one to another the large slabs to roof the souterrains, and the Grogachs herding cattle, we catch glimpses of the life of those who in long past ages inhabited Ireland.

THE REV. WILLIAM HAMILTON, D.D.[108]

An Early Exponent of the Volcanic Origin of the Giant's Causeway

"Here, hapless Hamilton, lamented name!
To fire volcanic traced the curious frame,
And, as his soul, by sportive fancy's aid,
Up to the fount of time's long current
strayed,
Far round these rocks he saw fierce craters
boil,
And torrent lavas flood the riven soil:
Saw vanquished Ocean from his bounds
retire,
And hailed the wonders of creative Fire."
Drummond.

These lines are taken from a poem, "The Giant's Causeway," written in 1811, when the nature of the basaltic rocks was regarded as doubtful, and many held that their origin was to be traced to the action of water rather than fire. Hamilton is rightly brought forward as a champion of the volcanic theory. In his "Letters concerning the Northern Coast of Antrim," published towards the close of the eighteenth century, he adduces strong reasons to show that the Giant's Causeway is no isolated freak of Nature, but part of a vast lava field

---

108   Reprinted from the *Sun*, May, 1891.

which covered Antrim and extended far beyond the Scottish islands. Nor does he confine his attention to geology, but fulfils the promise on the title page, giving an account of the antiquities, manners, and customs of the country. To those who care to read of this part of the world before the days of railroads and electric tramways, when Portrush was a small fishing village, and the lough which divides Antrim from Down bore the name of the ancient city of Carrickfergus, this old volume will possess many attractions. Three copies lie before me; two belong to editions published in the author's lifetime; the third was printed in Belfast in 1822, and contains a short memoir and a portrait of Dr. Hamilton. The latter is taken from one of those black silhouettes by which, before the art of photography was known, our grandfathers strove to preserve an image of those they loved. In this imperfect likeness we can see below the wig a massive forehead, and features which betoken no small determination of character. We can well believe that we are gazing on the face of a scholar, a man of science, a divine, of one who believed that death, even in the tragic form in which it came to him, was but the laying aside of a perishable machine, the casting away of an instrument no longer able to perform its functions.

William Hamilton was born in December, 1757, in Londonderry, where the family had resided for nearly a century, his grandfather having been one of the defenders of the city during the famous siege. Little is known of his boyhood. Before he was fifteen he entered the University of Dublin, and after a distinguished career obtained a fellowship in 1779. It was while continuing his theological and literary studies that his attention was drawn to the new sciences of chemistry and mineralogy. We can imagine the ardent student attracting around him a band of kindred spirits, who, meeting on one evening of the week under the name of Palæosophers, studied the Bible and ancient writings bearing on its interpretation, and the next, calling themselves Neosophers, discussed the phenomena of Nature, and the discoveries of Cavendish, or the views of Buffon and Descartes. Nor did his marriage in 1780 to Sarah Walker interrupt these pursuits.

Hamilton was one of the founders of the Royal Irish Academy, and dedicated his "Letters concerning the Coast of Antrim" to the Earl of Charlemont, the first president of that body. The book opens with an account of his visit to the Island of Raghery or Rathlin, where he was charmed with the primitive manners of the people and the friendly relations existing between them and their landlord. He examined the white cliffs, the dark basaltic columns, and the ruins of the old castle, where Robert Bruce is said to have made a gallant defence against his enemies. Here he found cinders embedded in the mortar, showing that the lime used in building the walls had been burnt with coal. This is adduced as a proof that the coal-beds near Fair Head had been known at an early period, possibly at a time anterior to the Danish incursions of the ninth and tenth centuries—a view confirmed by the discovery of an ancient gallery extending many hundred yards underground, and in which the remains of the tools and baskets of the prehistoric miners were found.

In a later letter a history is given of the Giant's Causeway, and of the various opinions which have been held regarding its origin. Beginning with the old tradition[109] that the stones had been cut and placed in position by the giant, Fin McCool or Fingal, when constructing a mighty mole to unite Ireland to Scotland, Hamilton alludes to the crude notions exhibited in some papers published in the early Transactions of the Royal Society. He criticizes severely "A True Prospect of the Giant's Causeway," printed in 1696 for the Dublin Society, showing how the imagination of the artist had planted luxuriant forest-trees on the wild bay of Port Noffer, and transformed basaltic rocks into comfortable dwelling-houses. The two beautiful paintings made by Mrs. Susanna Drury in 1740 are referred to in very different language, and anyone who has seen engravings of these will endorse his opinion, and feel that this lady has depicted, with almost photographic accuracy, the Causeway and the successive galleries of basaltic columns, which lend a weird and peculiar grandeur to the headlands of Bengore.

A large portion of Hamilton's work is occupied with a minute investigation of these headlands, and of the lofty promontory of Fair Head. A description is given of the jointed columns of the Causeway, whose surface presents a regular and compact pavement of polygon

---

109   See Letter I., part ii., edition 1822.

stones; we are told that this basaltic rock contains metallic iron, and that he has himself observed how, in the semicircular Bay of Bengore, the compass deviates greatly from its meridian, and each pillar or fragment of a pillar acts as a natural magnet. He also points out that columnar rocks are found in many parts of Antrim, and traces the basaltic plateau from the shores of Lough Foyle to the valley of the Lagan; nay more, he bids us extend our gaze, and remember "that whatever be the reasonings that fairly apply to the formation of the basaltes in our island, the same must be extended with little interruption over the mainland and western isles of Scotland, even to the frozen island of Iceland, where basaltic pillars are to be found in abundance, and where the flames of Hecla still continue to blaze."[110]

Hamilton argues, in opposition to the views of many of his contemporaries, that the vicinity of the Giant's Causeway to the sea has nothing whatever to do with the peculiar structure of its jointed columns, which he ascribes to their having been formed by the crystallization of a molten mass. The following are his words:

"Since, therefore, the basaltes and its attendant

---

110   Letter VI., part ii., pp. 183, 184. Compare with this passage the following enunciation of the results of modern geological investigation. "A marked feature of this period in Europe was the abundance and activity of its volcanoes.... From the south of Antrim, through the west coast of Scotland, the Faröe Islands and Iceland, even far into Arctic Greenland, a vast series of fissure eruptions poured forth successive floods of basalt, fragments of which now form the extensive volcanic plateaux of these regions." (Sir A. Geikie, "Geological Sketches at Home and Abroad," pp. 347, 348).

fossils[111] bear strong marks of the effects of fire, it does not seem unlikely that its pillars may have been formed by a process, exactly analogous to what is commonly denominated crystallization by fusion.... For though during the moments of an eruption nothing but a wasteful scene of tumult and disorder be presented to our view, yet, when the fury of those flames and vapours, which have been struggling for a passage, has abated, everything then returns to its original state of rest; and those various melted substances, which, but just before, were in the wildest state of chaos, will now subside and cool with a degree of regularity utterly unattainable in our laboratories."[112]

It is true that modern geologists would not apply the term "crystallization" to the process by which the basaltic columns have been formed, but all would agree that they have assumed their peculiar shape during the slow cooling of the molten lava of which they consist; thus Professor James Thomson[113] states that the division into prisms has arisen "by splitting, through shrinkage, of a very homogeneous mass in cooling."

It would be tedious to repeat the reasoning by which Hamilton, following in the steps of the French geologists, Desmarest and Faujas de St. Fond, establishes the volcanic origin of the basalt. It is true, he assumes the

---

111 Hamilton uses this word in its old meaning of rock or stone. He expressly states that basalt does not contain the slightest trace of animal or vegetable remains.

112 Letter VII., part ii., pp. 187, 188, 189.

113 See "Collected Papers," p. 430, edited by Sir Joseph Larmor, Sec. R.S., M.P., and James Thomson, M.A.

position of an impartial narrator, and brings forward at considerable length the objections which had been urged against this theory, but only to show that each one of them admits of a full and complete answer. Thus he states that the absence of volcanic cones does not embarrass the advocates of the system: "According to them, the basaltes has been formed under the earth itself and within the bowels of those very mountains where it could never have been exposed to view until, by length of time or some violent shock of nature, the incumbent mass must have undergone a very considerable alteration, such as should go near to destroy every exterior volcanic feature. In support of this, it may be observed that the promontories of Antrim do yet bear very evident marks of some violent convulsion, which has left them standing in their present abrupt situation, and that the Island of Raghery and some of the western isles of Scotland do really appear like the surviving fragments of a country, great part of which might have been buried in the ocean."[114]

We thus see that Hamilton clearly perceived that great changes, sufficient to sweep away lofty mountains, had taken place since those old lava streams had flowed over the land. It is true that science has advanced since his day with gigantic strides. Some things which he regarded as doubtful have become certain, and others which he regarded as certain have become doubtful, yet I trust that the preceding extracts will show that his account of the basaltic rocks of Antrim may still be

114   Letter VII., part ii., p. 194.

read with interest and profit.

As an antiquarian, Hamilton touches on the evidences of early culture in Ireland. He mentions the large number of exquisitely wrought gold ornaments found in the bogs, and translates for us a poem of St. Donatus, which, although doubtless a fancy sketch, shows the reputation enjoyed by the island in the ninth century.

> *"Far westward lies an isle of ancient fame*
> *By nature bless'd, and Scotia is her name,*
> *An island rich—exhaustless is her store*
> *Of veiny silver and of golden ore;*
> *Her fruitful soil for ever teems with wealth,*
> *With gems her waters, and her air with health.*
> *Her verdant fields with milk and honey flow,*
> *Her woolly fleeces vie with virgin snow;*
> *Her waving furrows float with bearded*
> *corn,*
> *And arms and arts her envy'd sons adorn.*
> *No savage bear with lawless fury roves,*
> *No rav'ning lion thro' her sacred groves;*
> *No poison there infects, no scaly snake*
> *Creeps through the grass, nor frog annoys*
> *the lake.*
> *An island worthy of its pious race,*
> *In war triumphant, and unmatch'd in*
> *peace."*[115]

In referring to the doctrines and practices of the

---

115   Letter IV., part i., p. 52.

ancient Irish Church, Hamilton enters on the field of controversy. It shows how widely his book was known when we find the *Giornale Ecclesiastico* of Rome taking exception to some of his views. This criticism led to the insertion in the second edition of the work, of a letter[116] dealing more fully with ecclesiastical matters. The reasoning, even when supported by the high authority of Archbishop Ussher, may possibly fail to convince us of the identity of the Church of St. Patrick and St. Columba with the Church of the Reformation; but we shall find abundant proof of the vigour and independence which characterized not only the early monks, but the Irish schoolmen of the Middle Ages.

Before this letter was published, Hamilton had accepted the living of Clondevaddock in Donegal, and had taken up his abode amid the wild but beautiful scenery surrounding Mulroy Bay. Here he expected to spend a tranquil life, watching over the education of his large family, and combining with his clerical duties the pursuit of science and literature. In a favourable situation for observing variations of temperature and the action of rain, wind, and tide, he pursued the investigation of a subject which had already engaged his attention before leaving Dublin. In a memoir[117] published after his death he suggests that the cutting down of the forests may have affected a sensible change in the climate of Ireland, and gives several instances of the

---

116   Letter V, part i.

117   See *Transactions of the Royal Irish Academy*, vol. vi., p. 27.

encroachment of the sea sand on fertile and inhabited land. Perhaps the most striking is that of the town of Bannow in Wexford. It was a flourishing borough in the early part of the seventeenth century, while in his day the site was marked only by a few ruins, appearing above heaps of barren sand, and where at the time of an election a fallen chimney was used as the council table of that ancient and loyal corporation.

When we read the closing pages of this paper it is difficult to believe that troubled times were so near at hand; and even when he wrote his "Letters on the French Revolution," Hamilton could not have foreseen that he was soon to fall before the same spirit of wild vengeance, which claimed so many noble victims on the banks of the Seine and the Loire.

He acted as magistrate as well as clergyman, and during nearly seven years he was treated with respect and confidence by the people among whom he lived. No doubt the majority of them did not regard him as their pastor, but they appreciated his efforts for their temporal welfare; we are told that the country was advancing in industry and prosperity, and remained tranquil when other parts of Ulster were greatly disturbed. At last, however, the revolutionary wave reached this remote district, and a trivial incident inflamed the minds of the inhabitants against Dr. Hamilton.

On Christmas night, 1796, while the memorable storm which in the south drove the French fleet from Bantry Bay was at its height, a brig, laden with wine from Oporto, was shipwrecked on the coast of Fanet, not far from Dr. Hamilton's dwelling. In those days the peasantry regarded whatever was brought to them by the sea as lawful booty, and were little disposed to brook the interference of magistrate or clergyman. We are told "that Dr. Hamilton's active exertions on this melancholy occasion gave rise to feelings of animosity on the part of some of his parishioners." This animosity was fomented by popular agitators. A stormy period ensued. One evening a band of insurgents surrounded the parsonage demanding the release of some prisoners, and for more than twenty-four hours the house was closely besieged. Two of the servants made their way with difficulty to the beach, hoping to escape by sea and bring succour from Derry, but they found holes had been bored in the boats, which rendered them unserviceable. Dr. Hamilton acted with much courage and coolness. He refused to accede to the demands of his assailants, saying he was not to be intimidated by men acting in open violation of the laws; at the same time, by repressing the ardour of the guard of soldiers, he showed his anxiety to prevent bloodshed. In company with a naval officer, he undertook the perilous task of passing in disguise through the rebel cordon, and returned with a body of militia. On seeing this reinforcement, the peasantry lost courage, and, throwing away their arms, dispersed quickly to their homes, so that the victory was achieved without loss of life.

The country now became apparently more tranquil, and in early spring Dr. Hamilton paid a visit to the Bishop of the diocese at Raphoe. He was returning to his parish, when the roughness of the weather delayed his crossing Lough Swilly, and he turned aside to see a brother clergyman near Fahan. He was easily prevailed upon to pass the night in the hospitable rectory of Sharon, and no doubt the visit of an old college friend was hailed with delight by the crippled Dr. Waller, whose infirmities obliged him to lead a secluded life. Probably the conversation turned on the state of the country; Dr. Waller, his wife, and her niece would inquire about the perils from which their guest had recently escaped. Perhaps they would congratulate themselves on the security of their neighbourhood compared with the wilder parts of Donegal. Suddenly the tramp of a band of men was heard. It is said that Dr. Hamilton's quick ear first caught the sound, and knew it to be his death-knell; but he was not the only victim—his hostess fell before him. Let us hear the story of that terrible tragedy as it was reported to the Irish House of Commons. Speaking on March 6, 1797, four days after the event, Dr. Brown said:

"As that gentleman (Dr. Hamilton) was sitting with the family in Mr. Waller's house, several shots were fired in upon them, the house was broken open, and Mrs. Waller, in endeavouring to protect her helpless husband by covering him with her body, was murdered. Mr. Hamilton, from the natural love of life, had taken refuge in the lower apartments. Thence they forced him, and as he endeavoured to hold the door they held fire under his hand until they made him quit his hold. They then dragged him a few yards from the house, and murdered him in the most inhuman and barbarous manner."[118]

From a letter written by Dr. Hall to the *Gentleman's Magazine* (March, 1797), we learn that the assassins retired unmolested and undiscovered. Nor were any of them ever brought to justice, although popular tradition, among both Catholics and Protestants, says that misfortune dogged their footsteps, and each one of them came to an untimely end. Dr. Hamilton's body remained exposed during the night, and was only removed the following morning, when it was taken to Londonderry and interred in the Cathedral graveyard. Here his name is recorded on the family tombstone; and in 1890 his descendants erected a tablet to his memory in the chancel of the Cathedral.

Hamilton obtained the degree of Doctor of Divinity in 1794, and shortly before his death he was elected a Corresponding Member of the Royal Society of Edinburgh. We have seen how he was cut off in the full vigour of mind and body—his last memoir unprinted—and surely we may echo the lament of his contemporaries, and feel that he was one who had conferred honour on his native land. Yet, while they mourned his loss as a public calamity, his friends would recall his words, and remember that to him death was but the entrance to a new life—the casting away of a covering which formed no part of his true self.

118   See report in the *Belfast Newsletter*, March 6-10, 1797.

www.ingramcontent.com/pod-product-compliance
Lightning Source LLC
Chambersburg PA
CBHW030021290326
41934CB00005B/430